# CIS-
# TEM
# FAIL-
# URE

ASTERISK: Gender, Trans-, and All That Comes After
*A series edited by Susan Stryker, Eliza Steinbock, and Jian Neo Chen.*

Duke University Press *Durham and London* 2022

# CIS-TEM FAIL-URE

Essays on Blackness and Cisgender

Marquis Bey

Printed in the United States of America on acid-free paper ∞
Project editor: Lisa Lawley
Designed by Courtney Leigh Richardson
Typeset in Garamond Premier Pro with Helvetica LT Std
by Westchester Publishing Services

Library of Congress Cataloging-in-Publication Data
Names: Bey, Marquis, author.
Title: Cistem failure : essays on blackness and cisgender /
Marquis Bey.
Other titles: Asterisk (Duke University Press)
Description: Durham : Duke University Press, 2022. | Series:
Asterisk | Includes bibliographical references and index.
Identifiers: LCCN 2021047318 (print)
LCCN 2021047319 (ebook)
ISBN 9781478015802 (hardcover)
ISBN 9781478018445 (paperback)
ISBN 9781478023036 (ebook)
Subjects: LCSH: Gender identity—Philosophy. | Gender
expression—Philosophy. | African Americans. | Cisgender
people. | BISAC: SOCIAL SCIENCE / LGBTQ Studies / Transgen-
der Studies | SOCIAL SCIENCE / Ethnic Studies / American /
African American & Black Studies
Classification: LCC HQ18.55 .B496 2022 (print) | LCC HQ18.55
(ebook) | DDC 305.3—dc23/eng/20211230
LC record available at https://lccn.loc.gov/2021047318
LC ebook record available at https://lccn.loc.gov/2021047319

For us. Yes, you too

# CON-
# TENTS

# PREFACE: CISTEM FAILURE

We are not destined to our lodgings, fixed from without, immutably. We are not only what they say we are. The criteria used to classify is insufficient, the taxonomy rife with fissures through which we can, blessedly, fall. I am ever romantic about the ways we move within restraint, a captive capacity that dissolves the captivity, letting us become in ways that might, who knows, unshackle the fetters fashioned by the captors. If only we knew we could move. Even when chained in the hold, on the gang, to the fence, there is always a little wiggle room. Room to wiggle, those minute tremulous reverberations, is when the trap gets worked and where the work is another way to say *I am (not), I am (not), I am (not).*

I was compelled to pen the words you hold in your hands, reader. Compelled, I say, by the gendered and ungendered, and *nega*-gendered, tugs on my subjectivity. The words' penning is the only way I can make sense of the thoughts, the feelings, the ways what has been called the body moves and lives in the world, albeit in ways that may not be legible quite yet. Or even in ways that are desirable for many. But the words had to be penned regardless. They are words that do not merely describe, as if they could; they are words that, as words do, inaugurate worlds. What I pen here is an attempt to make something else, some other way to be, real. And to do that, in the words of the late Toni Morrison, *you got to give up the shit that weighs you down*. My, and your, given gendered ontologies have been weighing me, us, down. So ultimately, though this will be terrifying, we are to give it up. And I mean that.

Breathe. It will be okay, I promise.

My compulsion can be traced to many moments and no moments. The tracing isn't what matters, as if finding a telos, a continuous through line, bestows validity. What matters are the intensities and bubbled-up moments that inflect something indicative of a tremor. One of those tremors took place in conversation, in sociality, where the giving of oneself in language to another is a way to emerge into a different subjectivity on coalitional grounds. This conversation with someone much older, with whom I had been meeting for the first time, was nevertheless a conversation with a loved one, a friend, a comrade. Kinfolk, as we say. She, whom I'll call "L," expressed the way transness both was and was not her narrative, a story that was hers yet not hers to claim. I beamed, its sentiments familiar affective kin. And I invited more, because I yearned for more.

L, a butch lesbian—an imperfect nominative, we both admitted—was gracious. She desired, like me, more language than what we have. She desired a way to hold others and ourselves lovingly in language, and shared with me, pointedly: if she, her femme partner, and someone like Kim Kardashian are all hailed under the rubric of cisgender, then something is wrong. *Something is wrong*.

*Cisgender* cannot capture some of us who are nonetheless hailed by it. Of interest is when the term cannot sustain the subjectivity it lashes against. What happens when one is grabbed by cisness, struggling to free oneself from its grip, wanting not to fall into other hands—even if one's own—but to fall, fall, fall? What happens when we, collectively, come to the realization that the way we have understood ourselves, and others have understood us, is inadequate—what happens when we can no longer pretend to the contrary that *something is wrong*?

BACK IN THE NINETIES, *The Matrix* was one of the most talked about films of the decade. Its innovation was impeccable, its fight scenes something my grandmother could watch over and over. Allusions and homages abound, from the back-bending evasion of flying bullets to the choice between the red and blue pills. I watched all of them, wanting there to be another world we didn't know of, a virtual nonspace where things were done differently. And honestly, that black and green color scheme was dope too.

Interestingly, something about the film went above my head back then. I missed it entirely. Who knows what might have been had I caught it, had I seen it as a gesture toward another possibility for how I could enter the world? It might have set my world ablaze.

> As Neo utters the word "change," a warning message—"SYSTEM FAILURE"—unexpectedly appears in capital letters over the program algorithm. The decryption freezes, but the zoom proceeds, the film's musical score holding a sustained string note that heightens our sense of what might next occur. Neo continues to speak as the shot pulls into extreme closeup on "SYSTEM FAILURE." The encroaching visual frame centers on the empty space between the "M" and the "F," those highly recognizable markers of legal and medical gender. As Neo makes the utopian claim of the speech, stating "a world where anything is possible," the virtual camera transits *through* the negative space between the coded layers of the "M" and "F" and into the blackness beyond.[1]

Cáel M. Keegan meditates at length on the Wachowski sisters, two trans siblings with the filmic gift of cinematic demigods. Muted radical trans politics and anticapitalist articulations emerge through their submergence. As the visual frame reads "SYSTEM FAILURE," the camera, as Keegan says, encroaches upon the space between each word, a space between the "M" of "SYSTEM" and the "F" of "FAILURE." And between the infinitely joyous and generatively tumultuous space is blackness.

What I missed was the gift of other ways to do gender, to undo it, to go in between it, to explore and excavate the abysmal blackness through and beyond gender's instantiations. What I missed, and what could have engendered me differently, or at least showed me that there was a different way to be engendered, was the trans, the *alternate space beyond or through* gender "where a new—and *black*—world, 'without border or boundaries,' might be instantiated." What I missed, and what I am grateful to Keegan for gifting me, us, with, is the failure of the *cis*tem, which is to say, *the fantastic end of the enforced gender and race systems that a post/racial trans* aesthetics speculates toward and pursues*.[2] What is facilitated when it is blackness that backgrounds, foregrounds, and facilitates system, and better cistem, failure? Welcome to the blackness beyond.

It is astoundingly striking, that scene, and it makes me feel something now, though rather late. I'm after that moment, that scene, as a filmic reel for my life. To transit through the "M" and "F" and into the black space is rich with analytic heft. The gender binary is the system, or cistem, structuring how we are believed to be able to exist. It is what we are given as the world, not understood as a system per se with all the trappings of construction and orchestration but as simply the way of the world. The success of a totalizing system is its masking of itself, its ability to hide its, as it were, systematicity. The successful system is simply there, simply what we have. That is the gender binary, and we have not been permitted to see its systematicity, its forceful, intentional structuration.

The system, the "M" and "F." To go between and beyond it into the abyss is to initiate the failure of the system. It touts itself as impenetrable, but how easily we traversed its interstices, how easily, indeed, we discovered that it *had* an interstitial space. Intervening in the gaps of the system that said it had no gaps, we have stalled it, or portended, at the very least, its untenability. What's more, that which invited us into the failure of the system, the failure of the *cis*tem, is an abiding, looming blackness. We are invited, then, to think deeply about the inextricability of blackness and cistem failure. It is blackness that resides in the cut between "M" and "F," not properly either of them, which is necessarily to say unable to abide its systematicity—blackness, in other words, promotes cistem failure.

What this treatise attempts to convey is how the cistem is as it is because of its exclusion of blackness, *and*, to be sure, because of how those who rebel against the cistem are invited into a dissent by blackness. Reading Keegan's reading, what you hold in your hands is a meditation on blackness as that which is disjoined from, which acts as a disjuncture relative to, which invites and initiates the failure of, the cistem defined by the impenetrability of "M" and "F." Extending this into realms of the autobiographical (how closely such questions nuzzle my own life) and the theoretical (how one has come to live the emotional life of ideas, those ideas that assert something new to know about life, or even to unknow about the life we have been given), you, reader, my companion traversing the myriad levels of infernal regimes of gender, will be trekking along a path lined with musings on the ways blackness and cisgender converge with, butt heads against, side-eye, and vanquish one another. If the failure of the cistem—the system of cisgender; the orchestral disciplinary endeavor to coercively cohere gendered subjectivity into a mutually exclusionary "M" or "F," deviation from which invites extermination, invalidation, and gaslighting—can be found in the effects of a blackness beyond, what is the relationship between blackness and the cistem? Might it be that those proximate to blackness invite the necessary failure of the system of cisgender?

Keegan goes to the end of the thought, conveying the constitutive blackness of the world beyond "M" and "F" where there are no borders or boundaries, of which the cistem is paradigmatic. When the failure of the cistem is impending, blackness is present, and the bringing about of the cistem's failure inaugurates the wondrous cessation of enforced gender. Which is to say, as is this entire treatise that lies before you, gender abolition. Blackness's antagonism toward cisgender and cisgender's normativity, its antiblackness, calls into question the very apparatus of gender itself as an organizing frame. It is a frame that does violence, that curtails. So it is not a matter of massaging the rough edges of the frame; it is a matter of disposing of the frame. That disposal is the concerted, worked-at failure of the cistem.

THE DRIVING THRUST is this, as inelegantly straightforward as it may be: cisgender is a categorical ruse disingenuously hailing those who nevertheless do not and cannot sit comfortably within it. It is a structuration permitting narrow forms of en*gendering*—the coming into being through and as gendered embodiment precisely in order to come into being at all. Cisgender requires a physiognomic comportment, indeed, but also a social, intellectual, behavioral, and interpersonal habitus in order for it to maintain its coherency and imply its naturalness. Blackness, in turn, is irreverent toward cisgender. There is a *queerness and transness that constitute Blackness*, as Jian Neo Chen would assert, meaning: *The Black becomes the aporia between sex and gender such that the two never meet in any fashion that would satisfy the dictates of normative heterosexuality.*[3] Blackness and cisgender, put simply, have beef.

The nature of this beef is what I am primed to explore. This is not a meditation on black cisgender people, as a misreading might offer as an expectation; nor is this an abdication of the hierarchies embedded in the comportment of certain bodies over others. I offer here a reckoning with the disjunction blackness initiates in the fabric of cisgender. Suspended will be a delineation of check marks and re-re-rehashed criteria for ire at the commonsense assumptions that bestow upon someone cisgender status. *I am not going to argue that the transgendered body has a material specificity that marks it as different from a normatively gendered body*, a cisgender body, for reasons that include the sliding, never-agreed-upon threshold for departure from cis and arrival in trans, as Gayle Salamon had in mind.[4] To do this would "assume a body," in Salamon's verbiage; it would assume a preexistent delimitation of the boundaries that clearly demarcate the cis from the trans. Cistem failure seeks the withoutness of borders and boundaries in service, unapologetically, of the abolition of the cistem's gender and gender's cistem.

There are many things that we already know. We can endlessly cite them in our articles, our monographs, in our Tweets and posts, our think pieces and blogs. We cite the radical feminist knowledge that *sex's difference from gender makes possible the account of un/alignment that constitutes cisgender and transgender as discrete and self-enclosed identities*. We cite that *whiteness is constitutive of binary gender as a construct*. We cite how we wish to be *against and beyond the constitutively white settler binary cis gender symbolic and social order*. We cite that *this problematizing of gender places her, the black woman, out of the traditional symbolics of female gender, and it is our task to make a place for this different social subject*. And we cite: *There is no body, no sexuality and, simply put, no sex outside the long history of Western imperialism's shattering of the world.*[5] All right, then, let's begin from here.

Might this require that we heed the possibility of cisgender itself being mythic in a way that necessitates a grappling with its mythos and putting pressure on the unqualified assertion of a material accrual of privilege? Might it require a recognition of cisgender's attachment to whiteness and, thus, its incompatibility with blackness in a way that troubles the blanketing of that very privilege presumed to be bestowed to *all* cis people? And might it mean that arriving at, or near, that Spillersian "place for this different social subject" will be a place that many of y'all may not be ready for, an abolitionist place that does not abide the trappings of legibility you snuggle with even when trying to bring about a radically just world? It can no longer be our end goal to say these things without considering deeply what they imply. Because it strikes me that it implies complete and total cistem failure.

In this spirit, *Cistem Failure: Essays on Blackness and Cisgender* is intent on mining the nexus of blackness and cisgender, its disjunctive relationship and, too, what the two might mean apart from one another. The essays herein are meditations, musings, prayers, and pissed-off rants about a regime that has curtailed all of our flourishings. The essays do not necessarily form a compounding telos wherein each cascades seamlessly into the next. Instead, approach them as a party crawl: "Back in the Day" has some actors and ideas and topics that start off the party; then, by "Heart of Cisness," the crew might have lost a couple people to the dope music blasting in the last bar or house or club, leaving the rest to hit up the next spot. And by "Blowing Up Narnia," we got a whole different cast of characters because everyone else dispersed throughout the night; but this new crew is driving the same car, texting the same numbers, drinking the same drinks, bumping to the same music. And it might even be the case that this preface and its cast make some guest appearances by the time we get to "The Coalition of Gender Abolition," as well as guest appearances throughout the essays. There is no straightforward plan or agenda for the night's crawl, only a shared impulse to keep the party going all through the night.

The essays will discuss cisgender itself, its fundamental characteristic as a ruse; they will discuss the life of those prescribed masculinity in terms of its constitutive and often overlooked and unmentioned, which is to say its assumed, cisness; they will discuss, sometimes, neither blackness nor cisness explicitly, but know, reader, that they are not absent. It is precisely when they are presumed absent that they are doing their most clever work. Know that they speak to and about you, even if you think yourself far from their content. Know that they bear on you; take that burden, for it is a burden that is intimidatingly relevant and, in its burdensomeness, monumentally transformative. But only if you dare.

# ACKNOWL-EDGMENTS

I've said this before, but I don't really like writing these acknowledgments. It feels disingenuous; it's hard to chop up, discretely, the people who have helped me in this book process. Because, to be sure, everyone has, people whose names I don't even know. Not to say that I'm in touch or in tune with all the beings of the universe, only to say that my interactions with cashiers at grocery stores and movie theaters impact me in ways that have, perhaps inevitably, seeped into this book. But I'll just write the acknowledgments and that'll be that.

This book arose out of an attempt to understand my frustration with a phrase with which I ultimately, save for a few nuances I'd make, agree. That phrase, "Black people can't be cisgender," often appended with an exclamation point and nearly always with a capital "B," frustrated me because I need more. I needed them to say how, why, what the implications were, where it came from. I could not simply snap my fingers or nod my head to its articulation, for there was something, I suspected, missing. So, this book is a compilation of the things I felt were missing, the hows and whys and implications and whences.

I could not have written this without the numerous conversations I've had with friends and colleagues and loved ones. I thank, in no particular order:

Susan Stryker, editor of this series, who first spoke with me at the American Studies Association's annual conference back in 2019. I remember walking up to you, Susan, after the panel discussion on the impact of "My Words to Victor Frankenstein." I remember you being so humble, but, like, actually humble, not fake humble. After the panel, I walked up to you and we hugged, a long hug that felt so loving and genuine. You invited me to talk after a meeting you were scheduled to have—a meeting, it turned out, with Duke University Press about the series in which this book is published—and we chatted for an hour about so many things. I was so thankful to converse with you, and you held me in that conversation so lovingly. This book is possible because of that holding.

And Jules Gill-Peterson, one of the not-so-anonymous reviewers of this book. It was you, Jules, I sat next to during the panel for Susan. And the day before I was on a panel with you, and you radiated in your awesomeness. (And Kadji too.) You were apologetic in the email you sent to me, after you got the go-ahead from Duke to reveal yourself as one of the reviewers, because you had never responded to my postconference email and the resources I sent you. But you didn't have to be; those conferences, especially for introverted people like us, I gather, are exhausting. But I loved the note you shared. I told my partner about it, about how loved and, to use our word for the linguistically uncapturable feeling of love, "squishy" your note made me feel. I was cared for in your response, and believe me, you grace this writing. I try to channel your spirit sometimes, a spirit of intellectual deftness and precision, like you demonstrated on that other panel we were on together—for Stanford's Gender Institute—on the TERF industrial complex, with grace. My conversations in your presence have been so crucial, you don't even know. I came to a kind of courage by way of yours. So, thank you.

I wish also to thank my partner, Sarah, for the numerous conversations we've had about so many things in this book. I sifted through thoughts with you, and you've been nothing short of the most committed thinking partner I could ask for. And not only that, all the other kinds of labor and assistance we cultivate together are foundational for this book as well. I would not have finished it or written it like I did if there were not someone to put away the dishes or, indeed, someone for whom and with whom I could put away the dishes, someone creating a space of comfort and life alongside me. That we share our spaces, physical and intellectual, means that there is a cocreation of the conditions for sustainable life that indelibly affect me. You are critical to that process, and that process is critical for the things that I do. And I hope to continue cultivating that kind of space for you as well.

There are so many other people and things and ideas I could name, and that I should name. I could and should name Jess and Danny, for the former has been engaging with me on thoughts concerning blackness and gender for the longest, and the latter is someone with whom I have felt the most genuine expression of family and kinship and who is quite literally in this book. I could and should name Treva, whose work and conversations over the phone have gifted me invaluable insights on what blackness does and how to live gender. I could and should thank "L" for the conversation we had that took the thoughts herein and propelled them into my life and writing. There are so many others, but to attempt to name them might be beside the point. So I wish only to say, to all of you, and you may or may not know who you are: thank you.

# BACK IN THE DAY

*Back in the days when I was young, I'm not a kid anymore, but some days I sit and wish I was a kid again*. Ahmad dropped this nostalgic slow-nod of a lyric when I was only two years old. I feel you, Ahmad, I wish some days that I was a kid again. There was something about back then that, I don't know, felt different. It's not some "Back in my day . . ." kind of thing you can imagine a crotchety old man saying, fist-shaking at the youths. I'm talking about that sense of newness, that sense of things not being rigidified. Which is to say, that sense of experimentation—mixing it up, mix-matchin' and mismatchin', being unenthralled with what has been said to be the only way to be.

Childhood is where a bunch of indeterminate, experimental things happen. Its indeterminacy and experimentation ground what I find to be a rich site of how stuff gets worked out, how stuff is newly known in the vulnerabilities of the working out of stuff. My childhood possessed a muted gender indeterminacy that glimpsed timid assertions of gender commingling with my blackness in ways unsutured from a presumptive fixation on racialized blackness and cisgender status, but were, terroristically, pummeled away from emerging. My childhood, I give to you all, is an aperture into what kinds of relations one can have with their gendered or disjoined gendered imposition amid crawling roaches and *heating up the house with the oven*, amid terror and albeit brief *joy in the noise*.[1]

I begin with the house. In truth, I cannot say it was a home, a distinction that rests in whether one can or cannot dwell, by which I mean—to Martin Heidegger's delight—to be at peace and safeguarded from danger, from evils, from precarity, and most fundamentally from precisely the things that might disallow the emergence of what is wrongly labeled one's "nature." I was housed, and surely loved, but I did not dwell, was not at home, I have to confess.

One's house is usually where one finds loved ones, and that was for sure the case with me growing up. But the house was also rules, codes of conduct, expectations, coercions—oh, the coercions. The house was not always a place of solace; it was, sometimes, a place of terror, a place of disallowance, a place that mirrored the very structures quelling me. The house was where I wanted my hair in puff balls (because that was a thing back in this century's aughts) but my aunt was taken aback, said that if I were to have my hair styled that way, the kids at school would chant *Marquis is a faggot! Marquis is a faggot!* The house was also where my mother, upon the conclusion of a news story where toddler siblings in matching purple PJs conspired together to break free of their crib, was peeved about her inability to know for sure the gender of these toddlers. *That mother needs to put them kids in clothes where I know if they boys or girls*, she said.

I have to begin with the house because, though coaxed into reiterating a narrative of especially black households as fundamentally good and well-intentioned, there was still violence. Dirty laundry aired, I suppose. The house did not permit some things, and I would have—and

I think many others would have too—loved if the house had cared for all the parts of me. But perhaps I cannot blame the house for its stanching of my gender nonnormative wings, or in reality fledgling feathers at best, because it was only doing what its architectural sinew demanded. In my small and quiet skirts away from alignment, I loved the unknown of what had not been offered me. Those skirted deviant movements of hair that I did not have or ambulations that were quelled with swiftness swelled the abode. They were glimpses of the "trans," and the house's violence cannot have done anything but do what it did: disallow those movements. For trans is an itch that things are not enough, a project of undoing, be it gender, institutions, the fabric of the social world; trans is *a project that cannot be haunted because it never tries to build a house.*[2]

Those invalid movements and desires attempted to build no houses or structures. They sought only a creatively generative process of unbuilding, a weaving of subjective modalities through, precisely, the interrogative. Another way of unsanctioned being and becoming through abolishing gender's tethers on my ontological stitches. Those movements and desires were that of an invitational and capacious transness by way of its setting aside of architecture—which must delimit and exclude in order to maintain itself, prohibiting entrance of the improper and unauthorized debris from the gloriously unruly outdoors—in favor of *anarchitecture.*

The anarchitectural, by way of Jack Halberstam, is a process of unmaking that loves the process of re- and unbuilding more than the outcome of what the house looks like. If we have the body as house, as architecture, the process of anarchitecture does not care much for making things work inside the existing framework, brushing off dust there and tightening a screw here; it is excited about tearing the parameters apart. And this, Halberstam says, departs from the masculinist tendencies of modernist architecture and brutalist styles of a will to instantiate power—phallic erections and whatnot (which is not the same as the mere likeness or possession of a penis)—toward not a "feminine" destination but, indeed, revelatory in the *project of dismantling and remaking*. As such, the anarchitectural indexes a certain orientation to the structural and purported rigidity of architecture. The building looks sturdy. It looks permanent, rigid, strong. And the building might get a new paint job or different decorations. Hey, it might even come under new management, changing the name on the front. But, it is presumed, the building is there, its load-bearing walls fixed.

Yet the anarchitect tinkers with the building and its logics of buildingness. That anarchitect—who I'm sure uses *they/them* pronouns (for now), I hereby tentatively decree—ain't building nothing, really, just tearing things down and messing with stuff so that what the building is to be is, precisely, that tearing and messing. Because what a building is can only be so much, is only permitted to be so much. So the anarchitect, well, they give glimpses of the things buildings can't be, insisting on what isn't and maybe can't be "there"—what has been necessarily voided in order for what is sanctioned to appear natural. And I like that. A lot. Because there is no fetishization of being at home or having a house to provide one with shelter. The desire for housedness is tweaked. There are other ways to feel sheltered and loved that do not rely on enclosing oneself in an impenetrable fortress. And maybe that desire that I had, inchoate as it may have been, is responsible for my infatuation with the trans, since transness, anarchitecturally, *offers an extensive vocabulary for expressing unbecoming*; anarchitecture, transly, is deployed *as a kind of wrecking ball that can knock and batter at the fortress of binary gender*. Unstitching the enclosure of the house's structural architecture is in fact more livable for some ways of becoming and unbecoming than the presumed house. I could not be loved, at least not all the way, in the house. It stanched too much. I needed more room than the architecture of the house could provide.[3]

But what else could I have expected? Well, I guess I expected, I demanded—I demand—that we, all of us, even if we have not yet emerged, be loved.

I still, despite all of this, wanted something else. I wanted the salvation of misalignment.

MAYBE IT STARTED with *The Powerpuff Girls*. My older brother, I imagined, was Blossom, his favorite color red and the oldest of the three of us; my cousin, Marcus, who had a bit of a temper at times and whose favorite color was green, I imagined as Buttercup; and I, the youngest, blue-lover and prone to lachrymose embarrassment, was Bubbles. Their fingerless might was awe inspiring to me, and the complexity of their interactions—love, anger, compassion, vulnerability, playfulness—was something I envied. It seemed even then that staying on this side of where I was told to begin and end meant I could not venture into other territories where emotional lives leapt gracefully.

The girls were one site of awe, to be sure. But they are not the figures of concern for me, even if I felt so strongly the sting of Bubbles being told "growing girls don't play with dolls" when I recalled the moments when I was told big boys don't do . . . whatever the hell "big" "boys" don't do (and, naturally, both Bubbles and I cried subsequently). What is most pertinent is the evilest of evil, the cruelest of cruel, the one whose name *strikes fear into the hearts of men* [*sic*]: Him.

Him is a Luciferian figure whose name stands for "His Infernal Majesty." Too, I'd say, Him is a sartorially gender-bending Satanic enby (Him's "Deviant Art" profile lists under the category "Gender": Male [*Or none*]). This is not to say that the show's creator, Craig McCracken, meant for Him to be identifiable as transgender. But this hardly matters most. Him gave us a villainous way to do and undo gender. With thigh-high jackboots, rouged cheeks, a pink tutu, pristine eyebrows, and a voice that swings from singsongy soprano to devilish bass, Him is unsettling. Unsettling to transphobes, for sure, but unsettling, too, because of Him's categorical irreverence. Him does not remain the same form; Him transforms sometimes, transmogrifies Him's body into a giant barrel-chested beast. In these instances, Him departs from the side Him was expected to stay on, and if that side came with it a certain gendered expectation, it follows that Him refused cis—on this side of—gender.

Him may or may not be transgender, but Him is certainly trans, in a broad sense—a categorical gender contemptuousness. So, almost literally, but not exactly, but still illuminatively, Him is a trans villain(ess):

> [Him] becomes hell-bent on destroying the rest of "the last vestigial traces of traditional man" thereafter. . . .
>
> The task of interpreting, and dare I say *relating* to trans villainesses filters out the flimsy tolerance that is contingent upon the ability to pass as cisgender, labor as an obedient professionalized worker in neoliberal capitalism, and rethread social norms through a tapestry of white supremacy and heteronormativity.[4]

Villains in *The Powerpuff Girls* are terrorizing the Powerpuff Girls as, fundamentally, "sugar, spice, and everything nice," that stereotypic characterization of little girls. Him, as villain par excellence, as a trans villainess of sorts, deploys a demonic gender devilishness to combat not just the Powerpuff Girls but gender assignation itself; Him, a gender-bender and a dweller of the *across, beyond, the other side of* (Him's home is in a netherworld, a fractured domesticity with floating and swirling furniture. Uprooted masses of earth whirr around unfixed, moving ambulatorily—Him, in a Luciferian overturning of the cult of true womanhood of the 1950s, is the *devil* in house); Him, a prince(ss) of darkness, a differently hued blackness, is *trans to gender*; Him, living beneath the earth, in the underworld, *is trans to the world itself and all its coordinates of being*; Him, a swirling irreverence regarding gender as a categorical fixation where viewers come to realize that gendering Him is never sufficient because perhaps Him is indexical of something else.[5]

I was off-put back then, just a tad, because I didn't know what to do with Him. Him was presenting something, emerging through something, that troubled me too much; I believed the things they told me were possible and accepted their coordinates of being—that to *be*, one must be either man or woman, and to be man or woman meant that you had to do man or woman. You could not do both, or neither, or something else entirely. Though Him troubled me, I want to believe that I continued to watch because there was something enticing and sustaining about feeling troubled. And that's what I am intrigued by: that timid inauguration into and through the troubling, a trouble Judith Butler called before I was even born "gender trouble," a gender trouble Butler, back then, for some reason could not quite call "trans." But I am calling it that now, and I am calling it that because the anarchitectural unbuilding is indexed in that language, in hindsight, of wanting something else. This is to say, I desired. I desired another way that was prohibited to me, and that desire, which manifested in enactments and speech and thought and politicality, matters. And it matters *just as much as any more observable social behavior like homoerotic sex or gender nonconformity*. It fuels how I texture my traversal of the world, how I engage others and on what grounds I consider engagement, what is permitted and deemed possible with and for others. That desire is both immaterial—which does not discredit its efficacy—and material, as it is unobservable yet is that which produces my methods of engagement. I desired the possibility of Him, and though I do not look like Him, nor do I have the same gendered impact on the world and others as someone like Him, to desire an outside and otherwise to the architectural lodgings you've been forced to bear is consequential. The enactment of transing permits identification *with people who were not in some observable ways "like" you*, so being trans to gender might express a desire, which fuels action—indeed, which *is* action—to engender modes of life unsanctioned. To desire and engender the undermining, the rejection, the subversion, the disdain for, the cistem.[6]

I didn't think then, nor do I think now, that in those moments I was transgender. But I gazed a little too long, smirked in shy affirmation at a murmurous *trans* as an ineffable longing and tinkering toward unsanctioned deviant ~~gendered~~ movements, desires, subjective tremors; glitchy subjectivity in service of a radical trans feminist subjectivity-as-politicality.

Subjectivity found and unfound elsewhere—found and unfound, maybe, in the social world that will emerge after the abolition of this one, a terrain that is still consequential and attendant upon our sense of (un)self even though it is not (yet) here. I was not and am not, now, in the pervasive sense, transgender, but it is possible—and, perhaps, imperative—that trans index a certain way of life unbeholden to the mandates of gender. Trans ways of life can be shared by people who may not have undergone affirmative surgery, who may not dress as the gender "opposite" to that which they were assigned, who may not use pronouns that "clash" with their natal assignation of what others might expect. As way of life, trans opens up affiliation with it on deeper grounds than the corporeal; as way of life, trans yields something radical in the relational, in the ethical and social, the ontological and epistemic. Trans offers variegated ways to emerge into oneself. Those variations of a self I knew not, a self that was foreign to me but deeply felt as kin, are what intrigue me now, and what continue to haunt me in ways removed and intimately visceral.

With one character, compounded by a smattering of animated behaviors and words from others in Townsville, *The Powerpuff Girls* gave me something I couldn't articulate back then. What it did flawlessly was insist on the possibility of being more than simply what was given. And that, just that, can be everything.

**I think you have to actually have a gender to be gay, and I don't think Frieza has one.—SoldierPhoenix, IGN Boards, 2014**

That might have all trickled into *Dragon Ball Z*. I was a kid who liked drawing, though my artistic form now consists of words rather than images. Any kid looking for cool things to draw found a trove of human and Saiyan subjects in the animated physiques of Goku and Vegeta, Piccolo and Cell, Trunks and Gohan. The ripples, the detail, all of it provided canvases to reinscribe into our own notepads, their spectacular worlds our spectacle to be reproduced on our pages, living their gorgeous monstrosity with each pen-stroke.

Aside from the illustrative opportunities, there was raised an identificatory question for me: the answer to the oft-asked "Who's your favorite DBZ character?" to which many responded, of course, Goku, was not my answer. I was not looking for the most powerful, most badass fighter on Earth or Namek. And though I might have tentatively answered the question on the grounds of coolness by choosing Piccolo—who I must say, y'all, is the blackest motherfucker on that, or any, show[7]—on the grounds of identification, however, or on the grounds of who provided me with an amplification of my subjective curiosity for possibility to become more than what has been given, was Frieza.

Frieza is, more than he knew, the horrible story. He controlled his own imperial army in Universe 7, feared by many for his ruthlessness. He is the primary antagonist for the third season of DBZ, it being known, aptly, as "The Frieza Saga." But he was more than all of this; he jammed the continuity of brolic DBZ fighters, giving kids like me, given to the nonmasculine, the queer- and trans-adjacent, different possibilities for living life.

His voice was the queer inflection for me. It was enrapturing, though for others in the DBZ fan world it was unsettling, an automatic scarlet gay letter. Frieza's voice, for me, was a welcome halt to the seamless trajectory of the Namekians' deep growl or Vegeta's too-cool-for-school timbre. Frieza introduced the valid commingling of a certain kind of toughness I would later critique, but nonetheless a toughness that could coexist with what is so often maligned as a "gay voice." To me, he sounded like a way out, an aperture looking out onto the grand gender terra.

He had four different forms. The first is what folks often remember, the puny-looking introductory form with "that voice." He morphs into a devilishly horned muscle-bound iteration that Vegeta calls, quite simply, "absolute madness." This form has that raspy, grainy, tough-dude voice so beloved by teenage boys growing into a masculinity characterized by anything and everything not-gay. His next form wasn't all that transformy to me, I recall. It was just another version of the previous iPhone: a bit more filigree, but pretty much the same, only now his head looked like that of an Omeisaurus. His final form, however, bucked final formality. Final forms are supposed to reveal the monster within, manifest the once-dormant beast just waiting to erupt and wreak monstrous havoc. But Frieza's final form: sleek, quaint, even. Like an adult-sized nubile baby. In an interview, Akira Toriyama, the creator of *Dragon Ball Z*, said Frieza's final form was purposefully made to look small and less menacing: Toriyama wanted to go against the expectation that villains and monsters become bigger and meaner-looking the stronger they are. This Frieza is sleek, unassuming. But the best part: his voice is back to its high inflection. At his most powerful, Frieza is not massive and masculinely grotesque; he is, if you will, thoroughly *feminine*. There was, for me, fertility there. That was a site, although villainous, for me to see another kind of strength and power not affixed to what my action figures looked like. I claim Frieza as transy kinfolk, affectively. He beautifully, ravagingly misaligns.

What many so often mistook for and imposed as "gayness" was paltry language. They had only the language of, definitionally, gender-nonconformity, which equals a man who desires sexual intimacy with other men which equals effeminacy which equals gay. But even they were off, so, so off. Frieza, I don't think was gay—but who knows; Frieza may have had a raucously, beautifully deviant sex life—because gayness disintegrates on Frieza. Frieza may not have had a gender, as Soldier-Phoenix so acutely and surprisingly put it on the Imagine Games Network message board. Frieza defied gender; Frieza, perhaps, didn't really care about gender—"gender" was not on Frieza's level as he was way too trans for that, too irreverent toward the ways gender requires linear and aligned form, being a good and proper subject. And I want to locate that as the site of my affinity, my love for Frieza. I must say there were moments when I rooted against Goku as the inevitable victor. I wanted Frieza, evil as he was, to come out on top, if only to show all those other kids I knew who homophobically encountered Frieza that he would not lose because of his departure from their gendered castigations, his departure from their expectations. And he didn't. I just wanted them to see that. Frieza's voice, his black nails that I want so badly to think is not their natural color, his darkened lips that I want so badly to think is not their natural color too—all of this made Frieza a force. His transgressions made him loveable in some small way.

AND IT MIGHT HAVE all resulted in my glorious meltdown with *Steven Universe*. The show is one of the queerest shows to have ever had eyes laid on it. *Steven Universe* allows chosen family to take center stage, nonheteronormativity to flourish, emotional breadth to stretch its limbs, and intergalactic kin to be forged through words and shields and fists and whips and spears. Steven and Garnet and Pearl and Amethyst express a subjective polysemy, a testament to the possibilities within and without, possibilities, too, within withins and within withouts. *Steven Universe* permits the validity of fusion. Beings the result of fusion *are the product of multiple Gems (or half-Gems, who can fuse with both Gems and humans). Fusions are formed when the participants are emotionally harmonious with each other. This state can be spontaneous, but it is usually achieved deliberately through a synchronized dance.*[8] Fusions, put differently, express the potentiality of one as more than their given ontologies—one can be and become more than what we've been given.

Which is why I cannot help but love, but desire as possible, Stevonnie. Stevonnie is the fusion of Steven and his best friend, Connie Maheshwaren. On the account of the show's creator, Rebecca Sugar, Stevonnie is intersex and nonbinary. "I am an experience," Stevonnie's Instagram profile reads, echoing Garnet's description of them—"You are not two people and you are not one person. You are an experience" (S1, E37)—"Intersex, non-binary, they/them," their profile concludes. I never really wanted to be the conflation of masculine and feminine, as if those are the only kinds of gender one could mix and match; much less did I understand myself then or now as being feminine on the inside, having some essential gendered core I was tapping into to others' chagrin. I wanted unheld and unbeholden subjectivity. A possible name for this is a gender identification not subject to the dictates of the gender binary or sexual dimorphism.

Such an identification, I think, is shorthanded in nonbinariness. They/them pronouns index this. For now at least. I've taken to thinking of and emerging through myself via the *they* and the nonbinary. At this time, which may change whenever the mood and sociopolitical efficacy strikes me. This affiliation with and usage of—not identification as or feeling that I am—nonbinariness is, at base, for me, a politicized gender irreverence. *They/them* is not really the "correct" way to address me; I'd actually be fine with being addressed by *he/him* pronouns, *she/her* pronouns, *xe* pronouns, *hir* pronouns—literally any. And, in fact, I have been, which is pretty cool to me. My recourse to they/them pronouns to describe myself is an attempt to mark my irreverence toward the gender binary, and to mark my tentative and always-in-process relationship to gender nonbinariness. Put differently, this is not to say I "am" nonbinary but, more pointedly, to say I seek a nonbinaristic relationship to my own understanding of my gender—an attempted unrelation to gender, as it were. So, it matters less what pronoun one uses for me; I am, ultimately, pronoun indifferent. That capaciousness is simply another attempt to express an irreverence and disdain for the gender binary and the ways it might inhere in pronouns. What I ultimately want to do is decline gender. So, really, use whatever pronouns for me that you want. Just don't *gender* me. *Don't you put that evil on me.*[9]

I can't lie and say that this is original; though I came to nonbinariness by way of a genuine desire to encounter the world politically, intellectually, discursively, and relationally differently rather than corporeally differently, I did also find solace and affirmation (and encouragement, to be sure) in Emi Koyama.

Koyama is responsible for really making trans feminism a thing. And for that I am already indebted. Via this trans feminism, Koyama bears a particular relationship to gender, one that is not just, say, an emphasis on transgender woman or insistent on the validity and importance of representing trans people positively in media. Koyama, unlike me, *used to identify as this gender and that gender, and even the neither gender.* But, like me, *nowadays she's tired of it all. "Genderqueer" used to work just fine when it was a non-identity, but now that there are communities of genderqueer people who identify with the label "genderqueer" it no longer quite applies.* There is something refreshing in Koyama's yearning for language that in fact fractures language inasmuch as the language we have is predicated on logics of staying on the side of the gendered world you were told to, and doing what that side demands. Nonbinariness, then, indexed in they/them pronouns (for now), is what Koyama explains as *not identify[ing] with any particular gender, but,* Koyama is keen to make clear, nonbinariness *does not so strongly identify with the state of having no gender to claim that as an identity either.*[10] Nonbinariness is the rejection of gender as an organizing apparatus for one's subjectivity. It is the refusal to be required to show up in the world on gendered grounds in order to show up at all. Nonbinariness is not itself a gender identity. Do not bring that mess to me, to us. It does not want your cookies, your pamphlets, or anything else you're selling, gendered world; it does not wish to hear your "Good" Word. It is too preoccupied with living in the world that this world cannot yet bear, living abolished (un)gendered life here and now, to your chagrin.

Stevonnie, then, is and must be more than positive nonbinary gender representation. Stevonnie, with their Gem-human fusion never before seen in literally any galaxy, is more than "representation" could do. We are not to end at representation; we cannot simply say that now, finally, we *see* a Stevonnie on TV, ergo, we've arrived. I don't even know if we can "see" nonbinariness. Stevonnie might be necessary as a beginning—but I'm not sure, the qualifying concession makes me uneasy—for

Stevonnie-like *representations do not simply re-present an already existing reality but are also doors into making new futures possible.* Stevonnie, representationally, *bring[s] new visual grammars into existence*, but it is the after-representation where things really happen, the new visual and haptic grammars made possible because Stevonnie, ancestrally, elder-ly perhaps, facilitates other ways of being—ways that may break out of representational logics altogether.[11] Stevonnie gives precedent for the first step in my departure from my human form, a form endemically white and cis and masculine. Before them, I didn't know that it was possible for Gems and humans to fuse, for one to be neither this thing they gave me nor the only other thing being rationed out. One could be, maybe, simultaneously, both and neither. And I get it, why they didn't offer this as an option. They made bank off of the two and only two choices. Who would want to go back to those options—which is really just one option, unchosen—when there is so much room to move in the options not given?

*Steven Universe* is not another show in which the boy protagonist befriends and eventually, inevitably falls in love with his girl best friend; it is not another show that nods toward "progressivism," throwing in a "Strong Female Character" to solidify its progressivism. It gives so much more, is so much richer. The Gems' shapeshifting gives mutability to our bodies, our subjective inhabitation. One is not confined to what one has been given. The seriousness with which mutability is offered as possible is a heels-dug-in rejoinder to the noise surrounding mutable life. Surrounding trans life. When they tell you, in the face of your nonbinary identification and they/them pronouns, "I identify as an attack helicopter," Amethyst *actually shapeshifts into an attack helicopter*. Like, OK, you identify as an attack helicopter? So do I, in this moment, and I take that seriously. Now where do we go from here? Where do we go from the taking seriously of radical identifications? From dis- and misidentifications? Rose Quartz believed deeply that all life is precious and worth protecting, and that must include the life of those who misalign with the implicit parallelisms that bestow life and livability. Life that looks like, yes, identification as an attack helicopter and, too, life that looks like a fourteen-year-old boy with a pink pet lion reminiscent in affect of Ash Ketchum's Charmeleon. Because perhaps someday long, or shortly, after the gamerdudebro throws out his identification as an attack helicopter in order to shut down your nonbinariness there will be someone whose livability is predicated on their, as it were, attack helicopterness. And I want to start to cultivate that as a possibility now, no matter how absurd, because today's absurdity was yesterday's transsexuality, and possibly tomorrow's attack helicopterality.

In the third episode of the fifth season we are introduced to "defective" gems known as the "Off Colors." No lie, I grinned super hard watching this episode, lounging in my mother's bed as I was home for the holidays and she was putting up Christmas decorations. The Off Colors live among one another, fearful of being found by scanners who'd detect their gems and shatter them for their imperfections, which is only to say their misalignment with how Gems are supposed to be. They live anyway, knowing that doom might be literally around the corner or down the path of a cavern. Their little space is where only those who don't belong, belong. How lovely is that? What is it like to come together with others on the grounds that you do not fit? The Off Colors belong together precisely because they do not belong. A promiscuous assemblage of things that are not supposed to live but live nonetheless. They are, as Garnet remarks in a different context episodes later, "on the outskirts of the possible" (S5, E15). And that is what it has been all about for me. It is where my grin and giddiness reside. Stevonnie and the shapeshifting and the fusions and the awesome gender play show what life could be like if the outskirts and the nonbelongers were our starting place. When we begin there for our ethical comportment and sense of what exists, we get something else. What I'm getting at is maybe more sentimental than anything: with all its gender radicality, its chosen kinfolk, its intergalactic extirpation of embodied common sense, Stevonnie brings to me, and to us too, livable life on the outskirts of the possible.

: : :

Again, I didn't think then, nor do I think now, that in those moments I was transgender. I didn't necessarily want to be Bubbles, my brother to be Blossom, my cousin to be Buttercup. And I didn't think we already were, because it was crucially clear that we were boys, had to be boys, had to continue being—which is to say becoming, painstakingly—boys, and boys could not be the Powerpuff *Girls*. I didn't want to be Frieza, nor Stevonnie. Yet still, blessedly, I felt for and with all of them. This was an identification of proportions monstrously small and exceedingly massive, an identification falling across professed and liminal and allusive genders but also, more deeply, an identification *through* genders into another gendered, another transed gendered or something-like-but-not-gendered, existence. When Bubbles teared up at being told "growing girls don't play with dolls," I felt kinship with her. I have been told, too, that growing boys don't play with action figures, growing boys don't wear their hair in puff balls, growing boys don't hang out with, platonically, girls. (When I first got a MySpace profile, curating my friends list, my brother instructed, "You gotta have you some niggas. You can't just be cool with girls.") I wanted to cry, too, and sometimes did, because people like us, Bubbles, we mourn the loss of those ways we were free and freeing.

While I was not, in those moments, transgender, I was, however, if I am allowed to say this, trying to develop a kinship, a coalitional solidarity, with the trans. I was made cis, and that which I am trying to emerge into is a refutation of cisness's hold over me. As coercive assignation as male at birth ([C]AMAB) creates the expectation of continuity, cisgender comes into being through a constructed declaration. One, irrespective of the assignation, inasmuch as the assignation is imbued with a sovereign divine decree—whether medico-juridical, or that of a deity—must do something with that assignation. What I did with that assignation was lament it, though I did not conceptualize precisely what that assignation was; what I did was yearn for unassignation, move toward nega-assignation through secretly moving my body and my hands and my hair and my voice in deviant ways, imagine myself as being more capacious in my stylizations of a burgeoning subjectivity. They made me cis, yes, but there were substantive moments—a substantiveness that amounts not really to the criteria that might traverse a recognized gendered threshold, I admit—where I rejected the making. There were moments when the cistem failed, and I intentionally, though fleetingly, briefly, chose the wrong answer, sabotaged my test scores so that I could see what it felt like to, not fail, but ace another test.

I'VE LONG DESPISED the "born this way" narratives. It takes on the logic of cisnormativity and the belief that the more long-standing something is, the more valid, the more true, it is. It says that if you have been such and such a way since a young age, that way must be what you truly are. And it makes sense that many queer and trans folks sought to adopt this language, as it made them more intelligible, more understood, and isn't that all we really want, to stave off our emo teenager-ness of "Nobody understands me!"? I in fact do not believe that I, or anyone, is born any particular way, if that is to be taken as having some legible innate desire or identification preexistent to and independent of the ways we are socialized, the language available to us, the other entities we have to interrelate and thus emerge in the world with and through. *I often say I knew I was a girl since the age of three or four*, Janet Mock confesses. But, *when I say I always knew I was a girl with such certainty, I erase all the nuances, the work, the process of self-discovery. I've adapted to saying I always knew I was a girl as a defense against the louder world,* she says, a world that required reckoning only on its terms.[12] There is so much tinkering and experimentation and figuring things out, so many false starts. To say that one always knew one was "trapped in the wrong body," a paltry and insufficient narrative, erases all the hours of sheer toil, the *years of passionate detective work* that are absolutely integral to forging, piece by piece, trans subjectivity. All the *pained questioning, theories formed, ditched, taken up again, revised, before finally somehow through the osmosis of popular culture, they arrived at the answer that they were trans.*[13] I, we, needn't say that we have known since the origins of our thoughts that we were not what they claim we are. We needn't play their game, adopt their rules and grammar, though I know that is a way we might be heard by them. But the interest here is cistem failure, and the belief in the increased validity of a claim the more long-standing it is, is, indeed, the cissiest of cistems. Failing the cistem and making it fail might mean we are permitted to simply say that while maybe we didn't know we were girls when they said we were boys, boys when they said we were girls, maybe we can be entirely comfortable saying simply I do not know what I *am*, but I know for sure that I am not what you say I am.

I surely was not born this way, which is to say on this side, cis, etymologically. I was very deliberately, very meticulously, crafted through violent means to remain on this side. I still rebelled, but not in conflagratory ways; there were few explosive or spectacularized displays of a femininity that belied how my person was conscripted, few sartorial manifestations of a femininity thought not my province. I have long been one of pretty basic bodily adornments, a choice made in part because of my lack of style but also, I have come to realize, because of a desire to refuse to announce in a clarion sartorial call on which side I fell. (Though this is in some ways disingenuous, as my basicness is largely read through a masculine vein understood as the lack of "putting on" something, a way to mark femininity and its adornments as added "frills.") But still, to be seen as being on "this side" is closer to a making-fit and further from a seeing-as. When Jordy Rosenberg writes, novelistically, *I am a guy by design, not birth*, I know he is speaking of a particular kind of trans masculinity.[14] But none of us, if I can say this in a way in which you understand what I'm suggesting—which some of y'all won't; some of y'all will misconstrue my words, which, I guess, is understandable—none of us are guys by birth: we are all, because we have been, at every turn, coaxed and goaded and pummeled and threatened and required to erect a very constructed architecture, guys by design. A horrible, awful, enticing design. I might be so bold as to say I was not born cis; I was made, diligently, maliciously, cis.

But what happens when you reject the making? What happens when we do not run back to the side we've been tasked with staying on? It is intriguing what happens, or what might happen, if we commit to wearing the garb, sharing the politics, having the tonal registers, speaking the language of other sides nowhere near this side even if we are said to still have an address saying that we are from and live on this side. It does not seem like it is even all about looking the part, as if there is only one part and as if there is only one look. It is not even about the address on your ID, because how many times have we gone to the DMV, presented our documents, asked if the written address is still current, and said no. Sometimes we feel ashamed, but how joyous is the feeling of having moved somewhere else, to somewhere unsanctioned by the regulative mandates of too-rigid identification documents? It's that joyfulness in the moving elsewhere that I'm after. Because, really, we are and must always be moving. That ID says I live there, at that address—an address on their grid—but, really, I am not always there. Right now, I am here, at this DMV. Sometimes I am in my car, on the road, which is where I might feel most comfortable. Sometimes I stay with a buddy for a week, crashing on their couch and eating Pringles while binge-watching reruns of *The Office*. Sometimes I am at work or on campus or at the store or running errands. And, yes, sometimes I am at the address on my ID, but I am in this room, then that room; sometimes I am in the shower or in bed; sometimes it is dirty or clean; sometimes the aroma lingers from the feast I prepared; and sometimes I have guests over, some of whom stay the night and some of whom forget their bags, which go into my closet for years. Is that the same address? It is not, then, that I want the address on my ID to "match" where I am because I am always elsewhere, I want to be elsewhere, unable to be *addressed*. And that's the thing that I am running, ceaselessly, toward, away from the address they put on my ID.

# HEART OF CISNESS

Gender, or sex-role assignation, or the clear differentiation of sexual stuff, sustained elsewhere in the culture, does not emerge for the African-American female in this historic instance.—**Hortense Spillers,** "Mama's Baby, Papa's Maybe," 1987

The cup of gender, trying to contain all that might be poured, runneth over with dingy tap water, spilling onto the floor, the table, down the cup's sides and staining them, eventually eroding the cup altogether. What is an eroded cup that can no longer hold that which it presumed naturally took its shape?

: : :

At the heart of cisness is nothing short of trepidation. In order to strut itself as natural it must obscure the pervasive gender variability in its midst, historically and contemporarily; it must erase and delete, back-space and strikethrough, the shifting loci that purport to be unshifting and not subject to temporality. But that's the thing: what cisgender *is*, or before (and after) its terminological inception, just "sex," is subject to historical vagaries. Constitutive of what is supposedly obviously one's sex/gender (often conflated, or, when not conflated, thought that the former precedes the latter, both of which are off the mark) are a swarm of different, and sometimes competing, criteria, from genitals to chromosomes to skeletal structure to societal role to corporeal capacity. This is all to say that cisgender just can't get its story straight.

**Moreover, he pointed out that if the warning to approach cautiously were to be followed, we must approach in daylight—not at dusk or in the dark.—Joseph Conrad, *Heart of Darkness*, 1899**

**I really wish I could say that white trans women are different, but on the count of white gender they are not.**

**I'm sorry to say that the word trans is frequently a misnomer. What you think is gender is really race. And that's the heart of whiteness right there, mommy.—Jules Gill-Peterson, "Communist Christine Jorgensen and the MILFS," 2021**

A secret of cisgender is that it is not only about gender. Gender is always a racial arrangement. We've only been deceived to believe the contrary; we got got, *we've been had, bamboozled*.[1] Do not fall for the single axis presumptions of cisgender, for doing so will woefully deprive it of the very mechanisms maintaining it. It is because "gender" functions by way of what Lacanians with a course or two of critical race theory under their belts might term "the symbolic order of whiteness": gender can do its thing, be what it is—which is, by most hegemonic accounts, binaristic—because its coherency is maintained by whiteness. Which is to say: cisgender is irrevocably, fundamentally antiblack.

Antiblackness, let's be clear, is not mere racism—or more liberal-y, "discrimination"—against black people. Antiblackness, by way of my dear colleague kihana miraya ross, illuminates a sociopolitical inability to bestow humanity onto blackness and black people, or rather those proximate to blackness (my preferential distinction); antiblackness denotes that *the relation between humanity and blackness is an antagonism, is irreconcilable.*[2] Cisgender is a categorical bestowal of humanity, a way to deem one sufficiently human by virtue of one's situatedness within the gender binary. Yet to be considered "human" is to be considered along a terrain that has constitutive of it a certain understanding of whiteness, or gender alignment, which then marks blackness as a darkness, one that stems *from the underside, the B-Side, the upside-down world of this normative, retrenched, dystopian, suburban, white, neoliberal hell that took hold in Thatcher's Britain and Reagan's United States.* In short, if I may be so forthright,

> Black gender is always gender done *wrong*, done dysfunctionally, done in a way that is not "normal." . . . This is why Black boys are hyper-criminalized just as Black girls and other Black non-male children are made invisible when talking about the issues of Black children. But instead of accepting the impossibility of Black gender as reality, and using it to create a different, freer, understandings [*sic*] of Black being, we are pressured to force our way into categories that weren't just not made for us, but designed specifically for our exclusion.[3]

Cisgender, gender alignment, will not save us, is not innocent, is not safe. It impedes the gloriously slanted magnificence available outside of cis's constraints.

I might be so bold as to say this, with backup from colleagues and mentors and advisors: if we hold to a specialized reading of female gender as an outcome of a certain political, sociocultural empowerment within the context of the United States, as Hortense Spillers writes in what seems like the only thing many people have read of Spillers (though I get it; it's a good read), we must then regard dispossession—which is to say, slanted, or head-on, an effectuation of blackness, that onset of improvisational intimacy and rehearsal of unruliness and unruledness—as the loss of gender, or one of the chief elements in an altered reading of gender. Which is to say, blackness, and those proximal to its work, bear a trans relationship to gender, leans as (trans)gender, is not necessarily transgender but, perhaps, trans to gender—all in service of kinds of gender that renounce, vociferously, gender as such.[4] What I mean here is that to be cis is to be proximate to whiteness, as whiteness underlies the coherency, binary, hierarchy, and regulation inherent to cisness. There comes, then, an overreliance on the cisgender/transgender binary to the extent to which one invests in whiteness. That is, as a logic of hierarchical distinction and exclusion, cisness posits a way of organizing the world that so many people, even people of trans experience, take up: assuming that to be nontrans is to, automatically, have gender privilege. But the antiblackness that undergirds how these binaries are constructed and reproduced in the first place is part and parcel of how cisness maintains itself by presuming universality while, simultaneously, casting some out of its purview to cleanse its impurities.[5]

A problem that trans studies has actually been quite good, though not perfect, at addressing—unlike its twin sibling, queer theory—is the flattening of not only trans but cis status. That is to say, cisgender is not homogenous, a homogeneity that is consequential for its very definition. The discursive production of cisgender has been inattentive, on the whole, to the myriad hierarchies and discontinuities within it that travel along numerous vectors—namely, race. There exists some recognition as to how sex and gender are constituted via different national, racial, class, etc., scopes, but it appears that when it comes to cisgender these recognitions get thrown out, all cis people being diametrically opposed to, and privileged over, trans people.

Knowing that gender, which means *cis*gender, necessitates whiteness, racialization—for my purposes, blackness—muddies cisgender identity. In the context of blackness, the wrench in such easy defamations of cisgender people as a blanketed demographic is white solipsism and a refusal to think the fundamentally altering effects of race viz blackness.

History bears this out. From captive Africans being shackled into the hull of slave ships and being taken into "account" as quantities rather than gendered subjects; to enslaved black folks' laboring capacity being designated metonymically by handedness (or, as a full hand, ¾ hand, ½ hand, etc.) rather than segregated strictly by gender; to Jim Crow–era restrooms being designated "Men," "Women," and "Colored," collapsing gender in the presence of blackness; to black lesbian nontrans woman Kadijah Farmer being kicked out of a restaurant bathroom because others were convinced she was a man, which is to say that she was disallowed the status of woman. It is to say that implicit in our understanding of cisgender is the requirement to adhere to, to approximate, whiteness. Bringing blackness to the fore in the discourse on cisgender does not simply shame thinkers of gender for their assumptions of whiteness as universal; it is not a plea to insert black and other racialized people into the conversation and let that be the end of it. The heart of cisness requires, as Conrad's epigraph attests in a different context, that it be gotten to in the daylight—that it can *only* be gotten to in the daylight, through whiteness, as darkness would prohibit arrival. To establish whiteness as necessarily subtendant of cisgender and blackness as a critique is to question the very notion of cisgender itself and, aspirationally, to undo the violences that inhere in cisness.

Thinking the darkness, the blackness, that must be expunged from the heart of cisness in order for cisness to achieve itself is a necessary thought for trans studies, as this formulation lays bare a refusal to regard gender as manifestly transparent. This allows us to eschew a *binaristic logic that might reify a distinction between transgender and cisgender, black and white*; it allows us to eschew the cisnormative and transantagonistic logics of recognition, which means that we must *not readily imagine that gender, in this instance (or any, for that matter), can be adjudicated by making recourse to the visual.*[6]

I am committed not to "race" and "gender" but to blackness and transness. It is because blackness and transness assert radical invention, so much so that what is invented cannot abide grammars of intelligibility in this terrain. There is then a *transitivity and transversality of blackness and transness, wherein making (sense of) the text requires contravening commonsense notions of the body*—in other words, blackness and transness do not "look" like a particular thing; rather, they dislodge the logics that structure lookedness.[7] Indeed, they assert other ways to be that do not quite "look" like anything in particular.

Black and trans profess a departure from the racial and gender categories that wave nationalistic flags in their names; black and trans, contra the nationalistic, border-delimiting exclusionary posture (black and trans, then, as radically nonexclusionary), do not quibble over unhelpful questions of who is or who gets to be but instead love and embrace *the otherwise genres of human not relegated by concepts of theological-philosophical knowledge of categorical difference*.[8] And I mean this so, so much. Perhaps dangerously so.

Sometimes I really don't like that this is what I think. Like, seriously. It makes things much more difficult. To show up, as I have, to the meeting or the group or the rally or the "all-black" or "all-trans" communing and feel tugs on your intellectual integrity is tough. You can't say that in fact the ways that blackness is conceptualized in this space, right now, in response to such and such blackety-black thing that has a very clear with-us or against-us kind of vibe, is not what you think. You can't say that blackness is more than that, or different than that, or paraontological to and indexical of that. Say anything but that, for we need right now just to feel the comforting chimes of echoes. And that's real.

But that is not the blackness that resounds all throughout this treatise or this series of essays, if I may break the fourth wall. Here, there is the commitment to

> black forms of life that anticipate and appose epidermalization, criminalization, and genocidal regulation. In the inexclusive mo-

> bile situation and idiom, to which we people who are darker than blue have been inexclusively given, our runaway history gives us this: that affirmation in and through negation, situated mobility, and differentiated presence is blackness; that blackness is generation's more-than-arbitrary name; that she is our more-and-less-than single being; that critical celebration of tumultuous derangement, of the constitutive force of dehiscence, of the improvisations of imagining things, is written in the name of blackness, on and under its skin, in its paraontological difference from, which is its paraontological differentiation in and as, the people who are called black.[9]

I spoke with a friend some years ago, a kind and thoughtful black dude with a degree in chemistry and penchant for doing cool stuff with machine learning. We spoke of blackness, this kind of blackness, and his initial incredulity gave way to a deep, abiding understanding. Not, I don't think, because of a profound cogency on my part but the invitational pull of a capacious, "inexclusive" blackness that expanded its gestural demand to all in service of an expansion, not a dilution, of its radical abolition of the violent tethers of this world. I spoke with a colleague, a black woman with the sharpest of intellects, about this very passage, who simply could not get on board. *Why*, she inquired, *why do we now have to share blackness too?* I spoke with another, timidly, about my very real fear of articulating blackness in this way. *People will hate this*, they said. And I know. *But I love it. This is the shit that radical coalitional work is talking about.* Even with all of this, from receiving support to thoroughly convincing someone to outright disdain, I am still scared and still not good at thinking this. But I must, I always say. I must because I cannot and do not want a blackness that is reducible to an apoliticized—or, easily apoliticized, a politically waifish—epidermis; nor can I nor do I want a blackness the exclusive province of a select few, as its radicality, to me, must be shared, proliferated, because why the hell would I want to covet something that might unleash the very world we seek?; nor can I nor do I want a blackness that is only accessible through a history of terror given to those who are "darker than blue" because blackness is not reducible to and thoroughly exceeds a founding (and continued) terror and, in fact, is the written name given to an open "imagining of things" that converges astoundingly with the abolitionist imaginatory jailbreak that must include all vectors of violence, taxonomic ontological imposition included, and exclusionary racial epidermalization included in *that*. I know what I sound like saying this, but I said what I said.

I know that cisgender is constitutively antiblack, and I diminish none of that. Nor do I diminish the antiblackness that many of my students and colleagues and friends and comrades rightfully combat. I'm just here for the spillage, as it were. I'm here for the understanding—my primary understanding—of blackness as not beholden to its purportedly formative anti-. I'm here for the blackness that is precisely the excess of that, and, as Fred Moten writes, *the apparent (racial) exclusivity of the (under) privilege of claiming this (dis)ability serially impairs—though it can never foreclose—the discovery that the priority of the imposition, of sovereign regulation, of constitutive correction, is false.*[10] The priority given to the anti- of antiblackness, the emphasis on and understanding of blackness as primarily and solely (racial) exclusivity is, in short, false. Blackness ain't got time for that.

And it is *this* that cisgender can't touch.

AS A REFERENTIAL TERM, *cisgender* was not promulgated until the 1990s. Proffered by trans activists, cisgender was a discursive critique of the commonplace ways of describing sex and gender as unqualified and axiomatic. To leave "man" and "woman" unmarked, these activists argued, normalized cisness as natural. In this moment of activism, transgender was a broad designation for all kinds of nonnormative genders and, furthermore, a signifier of dissident, radical politics. By this same token, cisgender signifies an entrenchment in medico-juridical, status quo gender beliefs—a definitionally conservative relation to gender and at best implicit acceptance of the regulative bulwark of the gender binary. Before this, however, proto-cisgender discourse arose in 1914 with Ernst Burchard's introduction of cis/trans distinctions to sexology. *Cisvestitismus*, or a type of inclination to wear gender-conforming clothing, was contrasted for Burchard with *transvestitismus*, or cross-dressing. Over a half century later, *cissexual* was coined by another sexologist, Volkmar Sigusch, in 1991.

But the first uses of *cis* as related specifically to what we understand as gender, according to the *Oxford English Dictionary*, come in 1997 on a Usenet newsgroup. In a thread for transgender support, re: Julie's Outing, someone wrote, "You need a 'pure transsexual' environment. . . . Everyone else, T[r]ans or Cis[,] poses a threat to you." In this moment not only is trans broadened as a more general category of gender expression but, as is the focus of the present essay, cis is linked (with trans) to the position of a threat. In a reversal of transantagonistic modes of thought that mark trans people as threats to national safety (of "our" wives and daughters, always), here cis is being marked—much closer to truth—as the threat. Cisness, in this late twentieth-century thread, carries with it a violent way of relating specifically to transsexuality.

It stems from an etymological root, that of the Latin prepositional *cis*, meaning, as so many trans studies articles and monographs will clarify—not to mention think piece after think piece, tweet after tweet—"on this side of," opposed to *trans*, "across, beyond, into another state or place." Cis, when attached to gender expression, defines a sense of remaining on the same side of one's natal (or in this day and age, perinatal) designation. The iconic scene of this designation has been the moment when a child is finally expelled from a pregnant person's womb and the doctor declares "It's a . . . !," capping the proclamation with a life sentence of gendered expectations. Now, however, the iconic scene is an elaborate gender "reveal" extravaganza, with colored cakes, confetti, melons eaten by alligators, or deadly, fiery explosions.[11]

The short version is that cis and cisgender are untroubled ways of being a gendered subject. With cis identity, it goes, comes no need to question or examine your gender because you have departed from nothing, your home's furnishings all remain tidy and unmoved.

This is all the typical, perhaps even safe, understanding of cisgender. People whose birth assignation is the same as, "matches," their current gender identity. There is, though, more to be plumbed in this description. What if—and really, truly, I mean what if, what are the possibilities of following this somewhat iconoclastic manner of thinking—cis were not so stable? What if the radicality of trans propels a radicalizing, not *of* cisgender, but *away from* and *a fracturing of* cisgender? What if we seriously consider blackness's (cis)gender trouble? We ought to know, if we think about it, that the distinction between cis and trans is a nebulous one invested with uncertain and competing political registers and sociocultural understandings. Like sex and gender themselves, there is no transparent criteria for when one stops being cis and crosses into an unwavering transness. What follows, in other words, when we heed that the majority of trans people have no transition-related surgeries, either due to lack of access or desire? What happens to *cis* when we note that *trans* does not seem to have a clear meaning, especially when we don't rely on medico-juridical criteria? What is the threshold, the line, clearly demarcating cis from trans? Can we think trans in excess of an austere corporeal opposition to cis, which makes it something like a *reckoning*?

This is essentially an interrogation of the "matching" implicit in the definition of cis as aligning with birth designation. Revealed in this, ironically enough, is that cisgender cannot hold the stability it claims to hold naturally. It wriggles under the weight of even a little pressure. The gender binary's terms—man and woman, and that coupling's hubristic bothness—are not transparent across time, or even within a particular time. Their meanings fluctuate; their meanings do not mean or, importantly, matter in transparent ways. To utter *woman*, for example, has never been a pure, unladen description of an extant subject that lies before me. *Woman* and *man* are, to use Althusserian language, interpellations: the terms "hail" subjects into the scriptural meaning imbued in the terms, forcing contortion into them in order to be legible as woman or man. And to be legible *is* to be woman or man, so the story goes.

These categories, however, are constructed. And please take this past lukewarm popular iterations of "gender is a social construct." Social construction in this context is not social con*strict*ion, nor social role nor social control nor social determinism. Social construction is not to mean bearing no import on one's life. It does not mean the same as, though it is related to, performativity of genderqueerness. Social construction does not disappear what we know as the material body, making any- and everyone capable of housing fetuses or producing sperm. This is not a treatise on social construction, which is actually quite bereft of a topic to me. I mean something that even those who deploy the phrase don't want to touch: if we are to understand sex as unmediated, as immutable, as just there, as the stuff onto which the baggage of gender is placed—sex, in this sense, as a coatrack—then there is no sex. If this is what sex means, it is not a thing that exists. Taking "woman" as a case in point, Denise Riley notes that *"women" is historically, discursively constructed, and always relatively to other categories which themselves change; "women" is a volatile collectivity in which female persons*—a terminology that must be pressurized and interrogated too, not assumed to be self-evident—*can be very differently positioned, so that the apparent continuity of the subject of "women" isn't to be relied on . . . and can't provide an ontological foundation.*[12] Put most forcefully, as Judith Butler has written in *Bodies That Matter*,

> If gender consists of the social meanings that sex assumes, then sex does not *accrue* social meanings as additive properties but, rather, *is replaced by* the social meanings it takes on; sex is relinquished in the course of that assumption, and gender emerges, not as a term in a continued relationship of opposition to sex, but as the term which absorbs and displaces "sex," the mark of its full

> substantiation into gender or what, from a materialist point of view, might constitute a full *de*substantiation. . . . If gender is the social construction of sex, and if there is no access to this "sex" except by means of its construction, then it appears not only that sex is absorbed by gender, but that "sex" becomes something like a fiction, perhaps a fantasy, retroactively installed at a prelinguistic site to which there is no direct access.[13]

Misunderstand me not: it is not to say, as I feel I need to repeat, that anyone can get pregnant or produce sperm, but that these traits do not map neatly onto beings we call *women* and *men*, respectively. It is fallacious to assert that only, say, women get pregnant precisely because when we deem someone a woman we are not assessing one's birthing capacities—we have no idea whether the being hailed as a woman can give birth, even if she is read as, or is, a cisgender woman—but are in fact "retroactively installing" our gendered evaluations into the presumed continuity of such an evaluation being indicative of people who can expel children from their wombs. "Sex" cannot pull its weight, nor any weight, for gender is what is always operative. One cannot "arrive" at sex as understood as unmediated and obvious. Sex cannot get outside of language, of gender, of investments and political meanings, thus "sex" as such, a coherent, systematized axiomaticity of the body that escapes reading, is not.

THINK OF THE *SIDE*. It is a territory instead of an attribute. The side, which has, intramurally, sides within it, is traversed by anyone who knows its location and dares to enter. On "this" side are not only those who have been on this side for years and decades, staking fences and flags on this side, proclaiming its singularity, but also those who have wished to leave but perhaps do not have a valid passport. On this side are those who have marked this territory as the expanse of the world, and they commingle with those who wish to raze its crops. Inhabitants of a territory are not all patriots. But is there a patriotism in simply not having identifiably left (an identifiability the criteria for which is subject to scrutiny)? Irrespective of one's desire to leave, to abolish its borders, to lambast the land's presidency and most vocal proponents, to wish to commune with others in other lands but unable to because of the ocean or highway or padlock impeding you, is one still, nevertheless, upholding the empire constitutive of the ground that props them upright? Irrespective of the desire to volunteer oneself not at all as tribute but as persona non grata, revoking the nation's protection-that-protected-nothing, and in fact engendered violation, even if in ways unseeable (as if seeing is the only way to mark the presence of something)? How can we forsake without leaving? Can we? How can we demand being engendered on different soil when all we are given—and maybe all we can ever have—is the crumbling silt beneath our feet?

There cannot be destiny in where we've found ourselves placed. Or, rather, thrown. It is not so accurate that, innocuously, *into this house we're born*, as the Doors sing, for the house and its architecture dictate what our bornness can mean and under what conditions we can be said to have been born and continue to live life. More accurately, as the Doors intone, revising their assertion, *into this world we're thrown*. Being on "this" side for those who rail against the patriots of this side is a having-been-thrown onto this side. Being born does not cut it, its language too passive and a disservice to how having been born cis is more truthfully a having been thrown onto this side. We have been hurled into this territory as a violent and forceful gesture to perpetuate a prevarication: that this side is the right side, the only side, the side you—and everyone—just happen to be on, nothing you can do about it, so rep your set. I call bullshit.

We are not born into the world; we are thrown. But our existence does not stop at the plummet. We are capacious in our understanding of how we can show up, so I urge us to consider that *we can also throw off our thrown condition*.[14] In the movement of cisgender's dissolution, the movement of departure from the stranglehold the cistem has placed us in, via behaviors and thoughts and desires and expressions of worldly articulation, we can texture and revise the having-been-thrown. Our bruises heal, we learn to walk and run, to swim and dance. We learn to move in ways unable to be contained by the territory we were told is the only terrain. When we walk, how do we walk? In the walk could be an agency over how our steps enunciate the beings articulating those steps, which is to say, we do not walk only in the ways they've commanded. That kind of walking is walking for another territory—for a deterritorialized territory. When we walk in that way or other ways, rebuking the totality of this side, is when we begin to misalign, depart from this side's cis.

But—this walk might get us killed.

> There is a story that came out around, I don't know, eight years ago. Of a young man who lived in Maine and he walked down the street of his small town where he had lived his entire life. And he walks with what we would call a swish, kind of, his hips move back and forth in a feminine way. And as he grew older that swish, that walk, became more pronounced, and it was more dramatically feminine. He started to be harassed by the boys in the town, and soon two or three boys stopped his walk and they fought with him and they ended up throwing him over a bridge and they killed him. So then we have to ask: why would someone be killed for the way they walk? Why would that walk be so upsetting to those other boys that they would feel that they must negate this person, they must expunge the trace of this person. They must stop that walk no matter what. They must eradicate the possibility of that person ever walking again. It seems to me that we are talking about an extremely deep panic or fear or anxiety that pertains to gender norms. Someone says: you must comply with the norm of [cis] masculinity otherwise you will die. Or I kill you now because you do not comply.[15]

The young man may have been gay, or he may not have been. He was thrown onto this side, where his body had been orchestrated via a gaze that disallows certain movements that do not sit well with this side. He walked in another way, a way that implied other territories. The locus of rage for those whose patriotism for this side was so intense was his "swish." His swish was a way of walking, moving his hips a bit too much for a boy—that is, from the perspective of normative scripts for those deemed boys, boys don't move their hips when they walk. Hip-swishing is what women and girls do; and you are a boy, which means you cannot also be a girl, so your hips must not swish. If your hips swish, that means something that cannot have meaning; it means something that does not exist. But you exist. So we, real boys, must make you not exist.

And nevertheless, this boy walked as if he knew, and gave not a damn for arguments to the contrary, there were other territories. His hips, on this side, were constrained, so he moved them outside of this side's limitations. This side was not enough; or, he was too much for this side. This boy was thrown into the world, onto this side, and chose to throw off that thrownness, like the stone-cold gender G that he was, that he is, in my book. But others wished to throw him back into his thrownness, which culminated in a literal throwing. And he died. That cannot be overstated, written off, or overlooked.

The boy died.

So as not to concede, though, that his death attests to a demand to keep this side happy, consider how the originary throw, then the subsequent throwing of the throw, then the following throwing back that culminated into a literal *over*throw are not equivalences, which introduces variegation. The originary throw and the final overthrow were *both* deaths. For the boy to have thrown off the first throw, which manifested in swishing his hips and maybe doing other things with his body—with his eyes, with his mouth, with his hands, or even with his genitals and his anus—is it not that when he swished he approximated freedom? Is it not that when he chose to depart from this side he left death only to, in the final throw, be brought back to it? In short, this side was not lush, was not life, was not so different than the overthrow.

"YOU AIN'T WON DICK YET!" he often yelled to get us to run faster, play tougher, lift more, harm more efficiently, during games, practice, two-a-days. High school football was, for me, a pit of terribleness. It was one site of this diligent making into cis. I only committed to playing those four years because I liked lifting weights, and the only students who could use the weight room were football players. Everything else was utter trash. Practice was trash, my teammates were trash, the coach—Coach Vo, we called him, his last name "Vosheski"—was extra trash, and all the terribleness of toxicity blended up into misogyny and violence and "dick-thing" masculinity (à la bell hooks) and the bullshittery of the whole shebang—straight, unadulterated trash.

Some of us joked about Vo's favorite phrase, saying, "Well, that's cool, 'cause I don't want any dick." On one register, *dick* is the crass stand-in for *anything*, or a crass substitute for the differently crass *shit*. But there are other registers, I suspect. Vo might have actually meant dick: to work harder and run faster and more vociferously do what the masculinist sociality demanded is to win, or get closer to winning, dick. I assume that *dick* is Vo's word for the phallus, and I assume that Vo required us all to be proper men, and I assume too that Vo's conception of us being and becoming men required no variation within that conception, which means that we were meant to be cis men. I assume, then, that this sociality became actualized the more we venerated and achieved the phallic instantiation expressive of it. Winning dick was to accrue tokens and chips toward the prize of an unwavering, unmistakable, pristinely aligned masculinity.

I look around the locker room, a range of bodily compositions threaded only through the common denominator of the presumption—which is not necessarily a confirmed existence—of possessing a penis, and observe the alignment of cisgender and masculinity and assignation of maleness. They taunted and jeered; they denigrated and policed all semblances of femininity, of nonmasculinity; they measured their worth in how many bodies piled up around them. Conquest, via violent means, was how we got our currency. That we were still standing in a cauldron of harmed people was enough to make us tout our fortitude, not realizing that we were the cause of all the harm. Or realizing it all too acutely. The chit-chat got more chattery as we lost favor, needing to restore our status. Jersey number 55 would masturbate clandestinely in the corner, quickly turning around to show us "the monster [he's] packing" before the mild erection wore off (his anxiety rising, possibly, because what if it didn't wear off?). Jersey number 50 would brag about how much he benched yesterday in the weight room, swearing up and down and side to side that he'd hit-stick anybody on the field. They were in pursuit of winning dick.

The threat that was "not having won dick yet" lies in the "yet." Fond of a number of gendered insults laced with misogyny, as is not uncommon for high school football coaches, calling us "Susan" or "Sally" to get us to act right; noting that we had vaginas when we succumbed to injuries; saying we lacked "testicular fortitude" when we apparently didn't hate the other team enough, clarifying, condescendingly, with *You know what that means? It means you don't have the balls*—the ultimate aim, it seemed, was to highlight a presumed departure from proper, aligned masculinity, coaxing us to scurry back, as vociferously as ever. We had not *yet* won dick, attained proper gendered personhood, but you might achieve it if you do as I say and pummel, malign the feminine, eradicate any trace of gendered impropriety from your vicinity. Dick is what you are lacking right now, and that is the thing that defines not only your masculinity but you as well, insofar as masculinity is your proper lot, the only kind of gendered subject—which is to say subject—you can be. Indeed, if you do not match up and measure up, align and possess proper and sufficient endowment, metaphorically and literally, you are not a person to me. You, as Vo said to us when we lost games or could not lift enough weight or run over enough opposing players or earhole our own, are nothing. Worthless. To misalign or deviate from gendered propriety, from, fundamentally, cisness, is to fall outside of personhood.

But to be no one, in this terrain especially, opened up so many other things one might be. To be no one is, perversely, blessedly, to be akin to free.

These people, called cisgender, these people were not, are not, my people (I do not care if you think they are; I refuse them, am not akin to them; *these are not "my people." These are not "our people,"* writes Laura Briggs, who caught flack for saying something that feels so deeply needed. *They stand against everything we are for. Instead of worrying about how to bring them into our movement, we need to get serious about the work of organizing in opposition to their agenda*).[16] There might be, and are, tears in the net where some of us fall through. Like L, my friend who refuses the accuracy of her butchness being hailed under the same nominative as her femme partner and the Kardashian sisters, I looked around the locker room and refused to conceive that the burgeoning, quiet but still present, timidly emerging gender-outside-gender of my sixteen-year-old self was that of these boys. Like L suggested, if we were all cisgender, something is terribly, terribly wrong with it.

I resent having been lied to; I was told, by you and by them, that there was a mound of evidence that I was, am, and will always be a boy, a man: the pronouns, the genitals, the Christmas toys, the clothes, the life trajectory. These were used to illusorily convey that any deviation was impossible and, too, undesirable. And all of this proved my cisgender; my cisgender was apodictic, so I was told. But I was lied to, and I resent it, and that resentment manifests in sometimes subtle, sometimes conspicuous ways, which moves me and moves us away from this category I was not born but made into. The category, its hubris, tried to quell a desire to step over and around, across and to the side of, the regimatic chasm that separated me from the girls, from the enbies and genderqueers and agenders. While my step is not others' step, my destinational desires and effects of that destination not the same as theirs, I want to hold space for there being a kinship in how we were given something and said *No*.

We were accosted by "Dudes don't do that" and "Real niggas ain't like that" and, no lie, "If ya dick ain't this big [he held his open-faced palms impossibly wide apart, a length only he, the implication went, possessed], can you even call yourself a man?" (Not only, apparently, did he win dick but was a gold-medalist at winning dick—look how much of it he had!) It is a coercive gender binary that orchestrates all of this, one that equates a minimum genital endowment with a proper inhabitation of masculinity, of manhood, able to pass go and collect all that it can reap. Cisgender masculinity—or, because of most of our proximity, epidermal or otherwise, to blackness, the aspiration to it, the erasing of its disjuncture between it and us, which catalyzed the intensity with which we sought to claim it through what scholars have long classified as black hypermasculinity—dictated the extermination of all gender transgressions because of its believed infectiousness. In that locker room, on that practice field, the binary was king, its alignment mandated for access into the space, a king that determined, with the ardor the cistem demands, what we are permitted to mean, how we mean, and punishes transgression of those meanings.

But some of us, thankfully, lost dick, saw dick as an undesirable prize. What, then, do we mean, and as what do we exist, when the system, the cistem, fails?

### The Vicissitude or Mutations, in the Superiour Globe, are no fit Matter.—Francis Bacon, "Of Vicissitudes of Things," 2020

It is quite dismal to believe that one is destined to be what they have been told they must be, forever. The doctor's designation of "boy" or "girl" so long thought to be the end of the story is decidedly not the case. And that inspires awe, inspires something like hope but much, much grittier—inspires a sort of hell-bent liberatory refusal of the violences that have been inscribed into us and that we've been told we must perpetuate. We do not have to be cis. Thankfully.

With this I do not mean that everyone must become trans or transgender. Far from advocating the aping of what we think it means to be trans, lambasting in transphobic form the movements and vocal affects and histories of transgender people, the call is to vanquish cisness. Because cisness is less (though not necessarily never) a specific metric of embodiment and more—much, much more—a manner of, as I've said, engendering and inhabiting the world, what is required is ripping out the heart of cisness. Cisness makes its living on performative behaviors that are consolidated retroactively into a presumed natural identity, an identity that is, the 1997 online thread writer made clear, a threat. *This* is what we must eliminate.

To *be* cis is much closer to *doing* cisness. Take away this if you take away nothing else from what I've prattled on about: the heart of cisness does not beat on its own; it requires arteries and blood and chambers. It requires the adherence to social equations of male = man = masculine and female = woman = feminine, sometimes by force and often by coercion. It requires that your body and their body, not to mention your manner of referring to them, be beholden to narrow parameters of movement, to constricted scopes of validity. It requires that you think of two and only two genders, genders that mutually exclude one another and are placed in hierarchical relation. It requires that you discipline any breach of the gender binary's confines into submission. It requires that your understanding of health, of normality, be shot through entrenched lenses of what kinds of bodies are possible and desirable. It requires that you posture yourself, your life, your loved ones, your culture, your nation, your very reality on the impregnable claim that you and everyone else be this way, forever and always, or else. This is what cisness means; it is a reckoning that we must, if we are to survive, reckon right back with. So, vi*cis*situdes.

*Vicissitude, n. The fact of change or mutation taking place in a particular thing or within a certain sphere; the uncertain changing or mutability of something,* per *Oxford English Dictionary*. Fond of quirky little neologisms, I offer you all this one, a term I wish to apply to the mutability even of cisness, a mutability that renders cisness not itself. Because cisness requires behavior and articulation of itself, vi*cis*situdes are the warping and making uncertain of the very certainty lodged in cis affective and intellectual, and discursive, performativities. Vi*cis*situdes, those mutational movements, do not fit, are not "fit Matter," in the "Superiour Globe" that is this side of the terrain, cisgender. It is to transmogrify movement and thought such that it no longer fits as legible matter in the world that cisness made. Vi*cis*situdes, then, mark the onset and uptake of an anxiety regarding how one has been thrown into cisness. The anxiety indexed in vi*cis*situdes is instructive for how one might deviantly deviate from its devilish destiny. Warping away from the demands of cisness, vi*cis*situdes posit potentiality as other than cis; it posits a potentiality in itself as a differently, radically other-than-gendered subject. It is the throwing off of our thrownness. Those of us who are not hailed seamlessly into trans or nonbinary status, those of us who are thought to be or have at times believed ourselves to be cis, must caress the vi*cis*situdes of gendered subjectivity. The quirky little neologism vi*cis*situdes highlights a wayward transmutation of the gendered subjectivity one has been coercively, nonconsensually given. If we are not destined to be cis, if we can move toward undermining the articulation of cisness, then vi*cis*situdinal subjectivity is a warping of the regulatory coercions believed to be consigned in how our bodies are understood. Subjective vi*cis*situdes make us bad cis subjects, cis troublant—unsettled and indecent, improper.

Perhaps it is a reach; perhaps it is a naïve hand-washing of the blood cisness has spilled of others who fail, or refuse, to live up to cisnormativity. I care about this, deeply. And yet I do not care, much, that there are certain bodies that are read as comporting, because the presumed body is not the breadth—not even close—of subjectivity, of even corporeality.

The reality of the corpus neither begins nor ends at the understood limits of my fingertips, my toes; what constitutes the body, and, importantly, what constitutes how we encounter sociality, is inclusive of so much more. And cisness must pervade those realms too. It does not claim, entirely, the body, nor does it claim, entirely, the expansive terrain that encompasses how we engage in encounters. In those realms, even if we make no bodily interventions, we can trans our subjectivities. Those realms, too, matter heavily in how we choose to support or radically, utterly vitiate the architecture of cisness. Those attitudinal, affective, sociopolitical, discursive, interrelational constituents of subjectivity and what we call the world can vanquish traces of cisness such that the question is seriously raised whether we continue to be cis despite the apparent look of our bodies. Vi*cis*situdes, those wayward extrasomatic ambulatory intentionalities, ask trenchant questions: *But what if we don't obey? What if we are simply unimpressed by the threats and the promises? What if we decline the terms of the choice?* Obedience, which is to say appearing and being read as cisgender, is never as straightforward as it seems because we live this identity in textured ways, minimally, as well as redact the coercive bodily induction via extrabodily means. In the redaction, the disobedience, what is being gifted is an acknowledgment of the beauteous bounty awaiting us in our disobedience, our dissidence, our badness. There is some primo stuff that occurs in the wake of our being unimpressed with what we are commanded to love and venerate. The key point, or the point I wish to emphasize, concerns the possibility of inviting another subjective and inter- and intramural habitus despite how we are hailed. That hailing is often, against our own desires and affinities, believed to be our official position, as if we wear a badge we cannot remove. That official position, however, *may be contradicted by an unconscious position which has nothing to do with hormones or reproductive equipment.*[17] What is the name for that contradiction, that, as it were, "unofficial" position?

This is what happens when we remove the heart of cisness; this is what it looks like when cisness is on its last leg gasping for air. Holding our perceived bodies-as-aligned, as-matched, against us is blackmail. But it's a bluff. We are called by radical political allegiances—by black radicality, by queer insurgents, by trans and feminist killjoys—to be bad cis subjects and articulate a counter-reckoning with cisgender. There is ebullient liberation in conceding that neither cisgender nor transgender identity are natural facts but political and politicized names for how we enact our subjectivities and engender the world for ourselves and others. The cisness of "being a man" and "being a woman" is compulsory, which means that it is a violation of ontological proportions. The only ethical relation to have, then, is one of impropriety toward cisgender.

This can take the form of repetitively stylizing one's body in ways that deviate from regulatory expectations of continued gender alignment. It can take the form of refusing, to others' frustration and discomfort, to assign genders to those who have not gifted you their gender identity—a radical self-determinative practice discursively manifested in "That person," "The person over there," "Joan said that Joan did it for Joan." It can take the form of activism to stop the genital alteration of intersex newborns, or teaching trans histories, or declaring "Black Trans Lives Matter," or never shutting up about the coercive social construct of gender, or whatever other way you can expose and puncture the heart of cisness. Just be sure to transfeministically do what you can where you're at.

Being a bad subject rebukes the tenets of and for the "good of the nation." The nation and its attendant baggage of nationalistic boundaries and exclusionary practices is the very territory into which we were thrown, told to think of as the best, the proud and true, the land of the free. Respect its creeds, established long, long ago; venerate those who righteously uphold its constitution: have these bodily comportments, possess this set of genitals, chromosomes. Being bad at this, however, implies a deviation from the goodness that characterizes most subjects who behave, those subjects who, in Althusserian language, "work by themselves"; being a bad cis subject, then, leans into a coalitional relation, a heeding of how our interrelatedness makes a claim on us, so if we are to be in coalitional solidarity with those who approximate transness as legible on the various corporeal registers of gender, this must place a demand on us to rebuke the inaugurative terrors of cisness: to *become with trans*.

When we nevertheless "match" by medico-juridical standards, we cannot concede that we are doomed to cisness. It is imperative that we do not. Do not respond to or recognize calls to behave in ways that index and proliferate your purported match; refuse to sanction the purity, the divinity, of matching. Being a bad cis subject, emerging onto the scene vi*cis*situdinally, marks a dissident gendered configuration that expands beyond the body and infects the body *politic*. If leftist politics, of which I am a part, has largely agreed that conventionally one who is not transgender—has not undergone gender reassignment or confirmation surgery, and has not declared themselves, explicitly, nonbinary or trans or genderqueer—is necessarily cis and must tout that identity and carry its privileges without a peep, it becomes necessary to radicalize the left. Because trans is a demand placed on the tethers of cisness, proximity to trans loosens the tethers, tethers that move every which way and loosen the hold one has on their originary violation. Join the ranks of those who bring about your destruction, for the "your" has been infected by a violation. What I wish to articulate is a being *with* trans, an emergence into subjectivity through the disintegrative beck of transness as not specific (altered) morphology but simmeringly mutinous (un)relation to (gender) normativity. At issue, then, is not *who is or is not really whatever but who can be counted on when they come for any one of us: The solid ground is not identity but loyalty and solidarity*.[18]

Being bad cis subjects, swirling around vi*cis*situdinally, is a dogged conviction to the possibility of being more than our given, our forced, ontologies. Being a bad cis subject means that we emerge into *a willingness not "to be"—a critical desubjectivation—in order to expose the law as less powerful than it seems*.[19] Sure, we are still hailed by structures and others as cis sometimes, and we might answer with a half-turn of our heads out of habit or a glance out of fear, but in the continued pursuit of being bad, of articulating gendered capacity and fugitive movement away from cisnormativity *despite* our hailing, we turn against the law. The law cannot hold absolute power. And in turning against the law, we overturn the law.

# HOW YA MAMA'N'EM?

There is a muted peculiarity to being thrown outside of a recognizability that philosophers would tell you is necessary for livability, for legibility, the two misguidedly conflated though certainly—via the sanguinary bellicosity of history—understandable. The outsidedness to recognizability is indexical of a type of subjectivity not currently known, an identity onto something the likes of which we ain't never seen. It is a type, to my mind—among others, of course—that can be sensed in the linguistic: a type alluded to by the phrasal iterations and vernacular swings found in propinquity to blackness. There is something there, flittingly, to be caressed and put on secretive display, if only for a brief moment.

Concerning this meditation are the various ways language seeps from black milieus and characterizes a different, open way of coming into being, a way given to the nonbinary and antagonistic to the cis, a way beautifully subjectively multiplicitous. Certain terms, turns of phrases, and gestural diction allude to a way of mobilizing the *they* similar to, familiar with, yet in swervingly skirted distinction from the word's use in gender nonbinary settings (though the two settings are not mutually exclusive). It is not that I believe, or have witnessed, black folks at the vanguard of using nonbinary pronouns for themselves and others (though, to be sure, I share community with more black nonbinary folks than nonbinary folks of any other racialized demographic); it is, instead, that the *they* of nonbinary genders and the *they* of certain ways of linguistic expression autochthonous within black sociality share something, some kind of other-mother relation where the two uses of *they* are cousins but not really, which means, of course, that they are family nonetheless.

*They* as a descriptor of a gendered identity uncontainable by the gender binary is not new per se, though its assumption as an identity by those who find a home in being unhomed by the binary is a more recent phenomenon. *They* has been in use in English, to conservative grammarians' chagrin, for centuries. It is not a twentieth- and twenty-first-century linguistic phenomenon, strictly speaking. As an epicene term, *they* has been in use at least since the fifteenth century. Later, it made appearances in the work of William Shakespeare, Jonathan Swift, Jane Austen, and other notable literary heavy hitters. In *A Comedy of Errors*, Shakespeare writes, "There's not a man I meet but doth salute me / As if I were their well-acquainted friend." Swift, in *Polite Conversation*, has written, "Every fool can do as they're bid." Thus, *they* as a designator of non-gender-specific personhood has a centuries-long history.[1]

Not until the eighteenth-century, in 1745, did the pronoun as a gender-neutral term come under serious fire. Ann Fisher argued that the universal pronoun, the pronoun for all, the pronoun to end all other pronouns for general use, should be *he*. That is, when referencing someone of unknown gender or speaking of general, perhaps hypothetical persons one should use *he*, a foundationing rationale for which being the ungrammaticality of *they* in similar instances. Fisher writes, "The Masculine Person answers to the general Name, which comprehends both Male and Female; as, any Person who knows what he says." The universalization of *he* took hold subsequently, no doubt buttressed by a pervading patriarchal environment. But this practice, while becoming pervasive until recently—a mitigation brought on by the feminist movement's insistence on *he*'s phallogocentrism and vocabularic instantiation of cis masculine supremacy—was never fully able to eradicate the use of *they* as a gender-neutral term for unknown persons.

Contemporarily, the pronoun has exploded onto the public discursive scene thanks in no small part to the agitation and principled insistence on its use by our beloved enbies (that is, "NBs": "nonbinaries" or nonbinary people) and other radical feminists. *They* has won out as the nonbinary reference of choice over *it* or *which*, as Samuel Coleridge would have preferred, and over neologisms like *ze/hir*, as someone like Leslie Feinberg would have liked, at least on some occasions.[2] Indeed, *they* has reached such a zenith that, in 2015, it was named Word of the Year by the American Dialect Society (ADS). Hegemonic societal doxa has long mandated, and in some ways still does, what Miqqi Alicia Gilbert calls "bigenderism," a pervasive understanding that prohibits variations, exceptions, or deviations from gender protocols. Such prohibitions are predicated on "common-sense" axioms: there are only two genders, genders do not and cannot change, gender identity is identified through genital shape, the gender binary is "natural," and the like. Nonbinariness and myriad expressions of gender transgression via identification with transness undermine this doxa, one that only permits certain grounds for life and livability. To undermine this, then, results in a staunch counterarticulation posing in fact valid alternative forms of being and becoming a subject that rejects binary, stultifying thinking—a veritable, if you will, "Nah, we don't do that over here."

At worst, nonbinariness and *they* pronouns are seen as faddish, a temporary sojourn in the hipness with which genderqueerness or not being down with gender is regarded; at best, it is assumed that nonbinariness is merely relational, only *in relation to the colonizer, to White culture, to Western, mutually exclusive ideals of masculine and feminine,* centering these *as normal, typical, the true measure of gender.*[3] Departure from both assumptions is necessary, as the former deprives nonbinary genders of a seriousness that can commingle with or without a persistency, and the latter disallows nonbinary as itself a(n) (un)gendered subjectivity marked not simply by the melding of masculinity and femininity but also as their excess, their uncapturable outside.

This essay expresses a radical subjectivity begotten by the blackness of the "them," or the nonbinariness of blackness. And it makes clear how blackness cannot abide the containment endemic to a singular body, a body required to be but marked as impossible to inhabit in alignment with registers of valid gendered personhood. So, this essay is more precisely an invitation to come sit on the porch and rap with it; or a beckoning to stay awhile and don't get going so soon; or an offering of home cooking so you got something in your belly before you go on off to work; or a loving, incisive, other-mother-working query as to *How ya mama'n'em?*

## For Uncle Tommy: 1957–2020

It's like my Uncle Tommy—well, my great-uncle, as he was my maternal grandmother's brother—and the way his very name reverberates elsewhere. Don't get me wrong, I have never really liked him all that much; he always smelled of cigarettes and Colt 45, coming around unannounced like a musty metallic-smelling black Santa in December when he'd let his gray beard grow and jokingly, on December 31, would say, "See y'all next year." But he was not alone, or, he was not just himself. My great-uncle, whose mother named him Thomas Miller, is multiplicitous. That is, *Thom is them. Thom'n'em*, and my great-uncle, Thomas, resounds across time and space because he, but not only him, all of us, in some regard, on some register not quite legible as registerial, is a them, a they. He is them because of the way *they just been socialized, deindividuated, shared.*[4] That's the kind of thing that's so compelling, right? When we can find ourselves to be more than ourselves, in a way that expands beyond and at a more formidable depth than there being "something bigger than us," we can tap in to the kinds of things we want but have been foreclosed from being gifted with.

If my great-uncle, Thomas, Tommy, Thom—which is also the name of a dear incarcerated student of mine, locked down for life, but with whom I share both a constant epistolary practice and sociointellectual practice—is them and they, he permits a capacious thinking about what it really is that the nonbinary is up to. He permits us to be broad and polaristically irreverent; he is given over to a sharing with us of ourselves that bestows upon the process of subject formulation the refusal of conceding that to be is to be discrete. If he, if we, can be they and them in a certain kind of way, that means that those whose genders express or unexpress as they/them/their are and have been sharing with us the possibilities for becoming otherwise than what we've had imposed upon us. For all my queer-ass nonbinary trans kinfolk who grace me with their kinship and coalition to demand, effectively, recognition as unrecognizable to the logics of recognizability—namely, the subjective inaugurating of the gender binary—is the gritty gift of showing us all that we ain't gotta buy what they selling us. Indeed, we shouldn't.

I am of the belief, which is much closer to an affective, visceral, archival knowledge, that blackness circulates in a loving open relationship with such gift-giving as nonbinariness. Again, it is not because I believe that black people are somehow more "accepting," whatever such a terminological rendering even means, of gender transgression or indifference; they, we, are not, I don't think. Black people, too, are subject to the impulse to venerate the categorizations that allow us to live, albeit marginally, precisely because we so often do not ourselves get to experience life. I am committed to this thinking, reader, listener, fellow traveler and thinker and questioner, because something else is going on in the shadowy underbelly of the projects that purport a monopoly on existence. Blackness might be said to be not a color per se, and maybe not even the axiomatic artistic thought of black being all color, but an *antecolor*, which offers the possibility of thinking (gender) nonbinariness as an *antegender*—these ways of having something that we ostensibly are, or have been told we are, and often believe and accept we are, stand in, in fact, for something a little different.[5] I'm reaching toward that other thing that is here, is us, not really but exactly.

Is it maybe that the nonbinary, maybe nonbinar*ies*, as coextensive with an understanding of blackness stalls the desire to succumb to gendered personhood? And gendered personhood is quite simply to say personhood. This identificatory project in its bad taking up of modernity's theorization is a trap, put mildly. Yes, a trap, a snare that we have gotten caught in but are now walking around like it's the skeletal frame of our bodies. Because it is. It is a terrifying and no doubt absurd project to wish to detonate the very thing that holds us upright, I know. I am pushing you, reader, whomever you are, to say hell yeah to cutting off your nose to spite your face. Now cut off your face too.

An absurd project but a necessary one, for our nose, our face, our ontological makeup conceal something else that we might have achieved, that we might still achieve, if it were not for the insidious project we have come to call life. What I urge us to do is rebuke the things that we are told we cannot live without and, indeed, *live* without them.

**This transitive expressivity of gender within blackness.—Brooklyn Leo, "The Colonial/Modern [Cis]Gender System and Trans World Traveling," 2020**

I promise this is not a distracted, unrelated detour. It is a swerve, for sure, but one that curves us toward an illuminative foray into the black vernacular and vernacular blackness my skinfolk and paraontological kinfolk utilize to nonbinary, cisantagonistic, radically open subjective effect. If cisgender necessitates a specific way of being in the world, that way is fundamentally, for the reasons you know and also for reasons you probably do not, antagonistic to blackness. That way is aligned, singular, individuated. This implicit and expected "correspondence" between sex and gender—if these things can be understood apart from each other, which they cannot—is no mere balancing of the ontological budget. The ledger is ripped and shadowed by Denise Ferreira da Silva's *analytics of raciality*—the tracing of the emergence of this thing called racialization and its effects on the conceptual arsenal used to develop understandings of human life: the eyeing of how the racial produced the parameters of ontology, what it means to be and think and exist, and the fusing of bodily traits to geopolitical regions, cultures, histories, futurities, and value, whereby *human difference is reproduced as irreducible and unsublatable.*[6]

What alignment—an etymological cisness—requires is discretion. It requires that this stay put and not change; it requires that this body look as much like it has for as long as it can, which ought to be forever; it requires that nothing said to be permanent changes; it requires that only one subject live in this body, only one group exist in this space, only one category be here where it was supposed to be. No mixing, no polysemy, no multiplicity. One, singular, linear. That is what alignment is, what cisness is. But I have been reared in a space and place, with a people and groove, in a tradition and by a world of thinking, that has had as its effluvial highway coalition, fracturous emergence, mutability, opposition, and un-/in-/im-/mis-/dis-/-anything-but-cis alignment.

Then you hear around the way something like *They ain't know no better* or *They trippin'* or *And they was like . . .* And turns out, it ain't but one person we talkin' 'bout. A vernacular, linguistic idiosyncrasy, this is—but it is more than just that. It is a matter of language, which is also a matter of being, or subjectivity, which is a matter of that which constitutes that subject. I am making a leap here, but the leap is fundamental to ushering in radical abolitionist futures—futures begotten by the black and trans radical traditions articulated by Frantz Fanon, by Cedric Robinson, by C. Riley Snorton, by Cathy Cohen, by Ruth Wilson Gilmore—and that leap, if I am being given the go-ahead to make it, is that this matter of language that is a matter of being and subjectivity that is a matter of what constitutes being and subjectivity is, here, also a matter of gender.

The "match" between sex and gender occurs through the question of blackness, as the unthought and unthinkable of cisness. Cisgender, implying its own self-evidence and knowability, presumes a sovereign consciousness that stands "before speech or signs" and has immediate access to their own sex/gender. Yet if blackness is nonsovereign—is insovereign, as J. Kameron Carter calls this paratheological blackness, or as Che Gossett calls this gender-troubling blackness—blackness cannot presume cisgender, cannot presume alignment. It follows, then, that blackness is the unalignment indexical of the refusal of sovereign discretion. All this means is that Uncle Tommy held something that all those given to an understanding of blackness—an understanding that is not sovereign, not discrete, not possessive, and thus able to have been given to any and all of us—hold too. He was fond of saying that the basketball game his favorite team (the Sixers; he was, after all, a Philly kid at heart) lost or the football game his team (the Eagles—again, a Philly kid) nearly won or the botched dinner or the disheveled clothes or the financial fiasco, anything to his disliking, was "a mess." He, too, was subject to this mess. His unshaven face or his worn-out sweatpants or his clunker of a car that he loved nonetheless was also a mess. "Can't be coming in here looking all a mess," he'd say. Yet he, they, we came in anyway, loved still. Which makes all the more resounding the assertion that the presumed shared terrain that cis/gender institutes to make coherent subjects, to make aligned subjects; that the hubris of the sex/gender distinction rests on a fallacy of *sex/biology as coming prior to gender/identity* "is a mess." And it is blackness, Uncle Tommy's blackness, my blackness, the blackness of the non- and insovereign primordial mutiny that irreveres the categorical taxonomizations we call ontology, chief among which is (cis)gender, that does the messing. That messing emerges insofar as blackness *uncovers the implicitly racist and classist underpinnings of hard-line categories of sex and gender.*[7]

The they/them at the linguistic register of blackness highlights a they/them, or a disrespect for cisgender and its coerced alignment, at the gendered level of blackness. If cisgender needs at its definitional base the presumed referential stability of "sex" in order to say that cisgender is the match or "alignment" of this sex with the expressed gender, the instability of *They ain't know no better* offers an ontological instability and misalignment. This instability, I want to highlight, destabilizes cisgender's, alignment's, hold over blackness. Blackness and its proximates do not conform, in language or gender.

**Truly, the singular plural *they* is an incredibly accurate means to describe the singularities present within the plurality of trans.—Eliza Steinbock, *Shimmering Images: Trans Cinema, Embodiment, and the Aesthetics of Change*, 2019**

It is not, and cannot be, my claim that there is something specific to and peculiar of the racialized demographic known as black people that makes it—them; us—more accepting of gender transgression and excess. Though, it is and can be my claim, asymp/totally differently, that *blackness*, and those given to an understanding of its anoriginal, desedimenting openness, its unfixing, is such that it invites the marginalized and outcast. In other words, if blackness has manifested sociohistorically by way of an *insurgen[cy] [that] constitutes a profound threat to the already existing order of things*, which is to say an openness to those who are said to threaten the purity of the hegemon, via the mellifluous "Come on, you too, baby" or the "If you ain't got nowhere to go, then you stayin' right here," it is blackness that then names the cultivating condition for radical subjectivity.[8]

What I am trying to suggest in a language that takes on the tenor of its source is how language spun through the annals of blackness by what we can tentatively call black folks, or black milieus, allows for another possible subject to emerge not simply when the subject is unknown but when the subject is "known" but not captured. In other words, they ain't gotta be unknown to be "they," and in the possibility of being they yet known, they become possible in another kind of way. This language of the they bears a shifted texture when arising from, as it were, blackness.

For the word to emerge from black environs renders it no mere pronoun but, supplementarily, illuminative of *a path toward a way of life between available language and the space of the "unthought" or, at least, unspoken*. It is, as Tiffany Lethabo King writes in a different context, an *extradiscursive and semigrammatical performanc[e]*.[9] The they of something like "Doing something they ain't got no business doing," a phrase my mother is deeply fond of—but where she encounters all these people in all these scenarios doing things they shouldn't, I will never know—plays a kind of joke on language. Language knows it can do certain things, and some of those things are all that can be done. But the they here, blackened and torqued, in essence says to language, *Who they think they is?*

Having grown up in this space, I've noticed a rich tendency at the level of phrasal referentiality. I sense something not quite the oft-quoted nonbinary, or more precisely in this instance gender-neutral, "Someone forgot their wallet." It is different and more than this. I grew up around blackness and black folks who used the term *they* as a descriptor of a certain kind of openness to subjectivity. Even when known, the referenced person can be shrouded by, and indeed engendered via, the they such that who they can be is unstitched from ontological moorings that have long fixed us into hes and shes. To query something like *Oh, how they been?* or alternatively, and notably expressive of black vernacular English's (ana)grammatical copula deletion, *How they?* after being told about Jimmy having just gotten home allows for the referenced subject a life unbeholden to certain constraints. So while the folks I grew up around were not necessarily saying someone was outside the gender binary, there is something to the pervasive usage of *they* that speaks to the presence of (gender) nonbinariness as intimate with a notion of blackness, and that functions in a way that effectively transes subjectivity, insisting that there are other and otherwise ways to be.

And it has, I think, generatively corrupted me. Being bred in such a cauldron has permitted an ease to approaching others without presumption.

As I learn indirectly of a friend's shift from *he* to *they* pronouns, it is the blackened sociality, I contend, that makes moving alongside, harmoniously, their pronounal shift easier. I have been bred in a space that is conditioned by shifts, by people who come into existence via a categorical shift—that is, I come from a people and environment who shift the categorical desire, loosening categorization which thus enables an irreverence toward categorical holds. The trouble Malcolm X, at the Audubon, noted he was born into via his blackness, and the gender trouble Judith Butler made famous through performativity, find expression in the use of *they* by my grandmother, cousins, and aunts. Reverberatory in the black and blackened *they* is a sort of mellifluously daimonic linguistic genius whereby ungrammatical iterations reconfigure subjective possibility. The radical inclusivity characteristic of black sociality, where black sociality denotes an edgeless edginess with the capacity to hold all, has endemic to it a transed modality expressed in its *STEADY SINGULAR LOVE OF MUTABILITY AND CONTINUAL SHAPE-SHIFTING,* to amplify the viscous poēsis of Juliana Huxtable.[10] Loving the mutable, the shifting shiftiness that slides in a pronoun, engendering someone's multiplicity, is our constant coalitional dislocation.

MY POINT, CIRCUITOUSLY gotten to as it may have been, is that the reverberation of *How ya mama'n'em?*, *How they been?*, and other interrogative suspensions of (gendered), knowable personhood by black folks has the effect of some kind of opening to existing with and through one another on nonviolent, intra-active grounds. It is a discursive nonbinariness begotten by blackness, I am submitting, that enables this. It seems ultimately that the nonbinariness that engenders the possibility for a radical subjectivity through blackness and its sociality amounts to a profound assertion to *come become beside me*, in the poetic incantation of Andrea Gibson, to suspend the ontological imposition for subjective opening, an indentificatory journeying that comes into itself with another, a being-and-becoming-with ostensible only when we recognize another's unrecognizability as the vehicle through which they become recognizable in a way not predicated on a violence.[11] And this plants seeds for collective, coalitional, liberatory life in pronounced opposition to neoliberal grammars of extricatory individuation.

It is fallacious to presume that individualism, or the belief in the benefits of individuation, is the ticket to our liberation. The goal is not to become singular subjects. *They* insists on coalitional desires to become subjects with others without assuming that we know others; it insists on a refutation of individuation. Allow me a pointed observation by Nat Raha:

> quick thought on the gender neutral pronouns "they [them / their]." its fairly well acknowledged that deploying these words, that reference a plural, is difficult to begin with. a key thing about collective life is overcoming some of that ingrained individualism sedimented into our minds and conceptions from growing and living within western (neoliberal) capitalist society. there's a multitude of ways how such individualism manifests in our thinking and language; but how might - say, a pronoun of neutral, or multiple, gender(s) - take a step towards cracking the fiercely guarded barbed-wire around the contemporary individual; more, how can we as trans*/genderqueer persons and trans[*]gressors of policed gender begin to challenge the individuality of an identity, and create a linguistic space that recognises & represents the contingency of our genders in relation to the communities, spaces, countries, cities, languages, etc., that give rise to them?[12]

The potential embedded in *they* and *them* lexically forsakes individualism, which laps up neoliberal logics, and forsakes the singularization of Jimmy, of Tommy, of Lydia and Riley and gifts them all with *them*. It is that commitment to collective life and coalitional sociality we be talkin' 'bout, that contingency we coax toward us because in it there is a refutation of immutable ontologization. We be we through they; we become we as a becoming. Whether via *they* as a nominative for known persons we wish to give more room to exist, or *they* as a nominative for ourselves in gendered excess, it becomes clear that blackness and nonbinariness give way to a radical, and radically opening, subjectivity.

Blackness's circulation with gender trouble and nonnormativity open up an aperture through which to cognitively peep the nonbinary, distilled into they, as *a metaphor for being free, for a grander ideal.*[13] It is about gender, surely, as gender is one of the chief modes of captivity and imposed, nonconsensual ontologies; it is, additionally, about how we come to freedom as an expansive-ass antecategorical invitation. *They* refuses to assert that someone, anyone, was who they were told they had to be before, and remain in the future. *They* frees one from having to be, allowing them to become, and, too, allowing the person who offered the invitational they as a (non)descriptor to become alongside the referenced they. *They*, in short, facilitates the coming to become beside me.

# NOTES ON (TRANS) GENDER

I am invested in what it means to blur the boundaries of who these analytics belong to, who they can—or should—describe.—**Jennifer Nash,** *Black Feminism Reimagined*, 2018

We will go where trans* takes us, looking not for trans people (or people who have legally changed their sex) but for a politics of transitivity.—**Jack Halberstam,** *Trans**, 2018

This body that I have, or that I am, or that I am said to be, does not readily give knowledge of itself. It is not as forthcoming as one might imagine; it dissembles and evanesces, betraying how it has been conscripted and made legible. This body, one that is mine only yet never mine entirely, always the product of mechanisms from without, confesses lies. And it confesses truths, though truths that do not register as such. And, still, it confesses nothing at all, but its silences are heard screechingly as things that it is not.

I refuse to hail this meditation as a confessional because I cannot, once-twice-thrice and for all, set the record straight on what (my) gender is and does. The confessional as a mode of truth-telling is compulsory, the compelling of a truth I cannot necessarily abide. Confessions are mandated of us in myriad ways, implicit and explicit; we are required to confess what cannot be tactfully inquired, to wear gender-conforming clothing, to announce our statuses in legal documents, to ensure that our names and discourses and politics and behaviors all align with a perinatal branding. Confess your gender, again and again, or you will be deemed deceptive—confess if you have nothing to hide. Be accountable, the coaxed confession demands, to our *set of gendered norms* and *euphemistically display your concealed moral (genital) sex.*[1] Through a compelled (or, more accurately, coerced) confession of these innermost truths, the very notion of a gendered truth—that there is one, and only one, unchangeable and continuous, gender within me—becomes the means by which I am permitted to be someone worthy of another's consideration.

I want to negate this, not because truth-telling matters not, but because I cannot confess something that is not entirely, not really, not at all true.

The topic at hand is a peculiar one, peculiar because of its paradoxical dishonest truthfulness. Broadly, the topic at hand is my relationship to what I can only at the moment understand as (trans)gender, a testament to the intimacy yet distinction that accompanies my asymptotic treading of the line—thick as it may be, which some might deem as prohibiting my flirtation with the "trans" of (trans)gender—nebulously between "cis" and "trans." And, too, others' relationships to me as I tread said line. It is a tricky thing, to be sure, trying to assume without offending, or trying to inquire without conspicuousness, one's gender. It is a trickiness I know well, though surely not nearly as well as others who are more legible as people of trans experience, some of whom I share social and intellectual space with, and some of whom have gifted me, graciously, with a recounting of those experiences. The trickiness can often be glimpsed in a brief hesitation before voicing a *He* or *She*, and very rarely, in my experience, has *They* or *Ze* even been thought to be a possibility. It can be glimpsed in the jarring shift to "gender talk," or the mentioning of this gender studies class one has taken, this friend of a friend of an acquaintance who transitioned, this "problematic" (the well-meaning liberal's favorite catchall for the not sufficiently "PC") policy the president has just instituted. It can be glimpsed, too, in the smoke-thick palpability of discomfiture.

You see, I am a scholar and thinker, which manifest through the word, of transgender studies, among other things. What I express on the page, on blogs, on Twitter feeds—not to mention in person, interpersonally—is expressive of a political ensemble. But because of this work, it is often assumed that I identify as transgender. Simply by virtue of the work that I do, work that entails writing about transgender life, advocating for trans communities, and interrogating gender from a trans feminist perspective, there is the assumption that *who else* would be doing all this but people who are themselves trans?

What follows is a sort of entangling myself into the project, the yearning, for life toward gender abolition. What follows is how I might have had experiences that are given to a sensoria lusciously infected by trans's mobilization of fissures and fractures, making this, making me, ***not here to confess, but to confect.***[2]

THE "TRANS" OF "trans studies" is growing to be understood as more than the designation of a certain embodied identity the limits and contours of which we know clearly and definitely. That is to say, "trans" is growing to mean more than what we've nebulously cobbled together as an identifiable, true-blue transgender person. So as not to get caught up out here, I want to make clear that surely this does not dismiss the effects, experiences, or meanings of being transgender. To identify as, and be identified as, transgender indeed has a life trajectory and experiential knowledge that cannot be replicated by those who are not, generally speaking, transgender. Mostly.

My suggestion is one that recognizes the prefixal nature of the trans in trans studies. That is, a prefix, if you'll remember from grade school grammar lessons in your language arts classes, is an affix placed before a word stem, modifying it, working it, and making it do and mean differently. Over here in trans studies where we are, in consultation with academic and nonacademic trans folks, putting in work to think deeply about gender, we are committing, slowly but surely, to what is being called the prefixal trans. That prefixal trans changes the game; it makes trans modificatory, and ultimately obliteratory, of roots and rootedness. Which gives it over to a way of being unable to be hemmed by syntactical dictates. A way of being and doing that is, (im)properly speaking, a politics. It is not, then, a specific body or manner of dress or anatomical configuration. Because, indeed, how would one "be" an insurrectionary prefix? One can't, really. And one needn't.

I am following zealously the acumen of a number of folks in the field, folks whom I have sat enraptured listening to at podiums, folks who have hugged me to calm my nerves before giving my own talks at said podiums, folks I've texted after the Orlando nightclub shootings to send love and coalitional vibes, folks I've read every published word of. For one of those folks, trans as a gesture of identification is a way *to open the term up to unfolding categories of being organized around but not confined to forms of gender variance*. Trans, prefixally, *refus[es] to situate transition in relation to a destination, a final form, a specific shape, or an established configuration of desire and identity*.[3] Relatedly, for another one of those folks, trans is meant

> not to refer to one particular identity or way of being embodied but rather as an umbrella term for a wide variety of bodily effects that disrupt or denaturalize heteronormatively constructed linkages between an individual's anatomy at birth, a nonconsensually as-

> signed gender category, psychical identifications with sexed body images and/or gendered subject positions, and the performance of specifically gendered social, sexual, or kinship functions.[4]

In these ways, trans is not merely, or even primarily, about having a certain bodily expression or sexed history. Rather, trans marks the ways that one *transes* gender, how one relates to the normativity of the gender binary in subversive and critical ways.

But why? Why seek to broaden what so rightfully belongs to certain identifiable people? Why try to take this too from people historically marginalized? Part of my insistence, an insistence that leads to the iconoclasm and controversiality that will soon follow, comes from C. Riley Snorton, who asserts unwaveringly that *one should not readily imagine that gender, in this instance (or any, for that matter), can be adjudicated by making recourse to the visual.*[5] If we are to commit to gender self-determination, which is a condition of queer, abolitionist emergence, and if we are to commit to a radical world (dis)order in terms of gender, which necessitates the overthrowing of hegemonic gender impositions, we must refuse to assume that we can detect, before its revelation, another's gender simply by looking at them.

**Sexual dimorphism has been an important characteristic of what I call "the light side" of the colonial/modern gender system. Those in the "dark side" were not necessarily understood dimorphically.—María Lugones, "The Coloniality of Gender," 2008**

It is important, too, as any person devoted to intersectionality will vehemently insist, that race is also an impacting factor here. Or, put clearly, race—and here I am thinking specifically of blackness, as racial, extra-racial, and anteracial—subtends gender as a vector through which people (and nonpeople, to be sure) become legible *as people* in the world. It impacts gender in a way that highlights how what we understand as gender is predicated on certain racial elisions. In other words, "gender" properly understood has long been indebted to, constituted by, expressive of a proximity to whiteness. Gender and the meanings attached to it are always and already racialized meanings; thus I cannot meditate on meanings of gender without also addressing racialized gender discourses, especially as they pertain to (my) blackness.

Consider the ways that, as detailed by C. Riley Snorton, enslaved black people with vesicovaginal fistula—a complication of obstructed childbirth—were operated on by James Marion Sims. The procedures entailed close observation of genitalia in a public setting, indeed staged and put on display by Sims to allow other medical practitioners to view the vaginas of these enslaved black people. For Sims to spend three years operating on enslaved chattel persons during this era reveals how race-cum-blackness rests at the foundation of biologized conceptions of sex and gender. In other words, if Sims utilized enslaved, imprisoned black people to develop the *key to restoring a woman's health*, and if white femininity—which is, properly speaking, to say womanhood—*is conferred in relation to an unwillingness to view white female genitalia*, then the people being operated on were not understood under the heading of "woman."[6] Blackness disintegrates the coherence of gender as a category amenable to blackness.

Consider how, in the early and mid-twentieth century, during Jim and Jane Crow, the site of the bathroom housed the simultaneity of racial *and* gender anxieties, collapsing gender in the presence of racialized, black subjectivity. Time-travel for a second, gaze at a public institution with segregated bathrooms, observe what is and is not said. What do you see? "Men's," "Women's," and—pay close attention—"Colored." The "Men's" and "Women's" is coded with an underlying, even enabling, whiteness. Racialized identity is prohibited gender distinction, and if I can be allowed to think about this racialization as potent with blackness in this era in which black/white relations are so intense, then "gender," as binaristically sanctioned, is off-limits for blackness. Gender breaks, collapses in on itself, where blackness is concerned. There is, thus, a deeply insidious overlapping of transantagonism and antiblackness such that blackness is radical, transgressive kin with transness. As Toby Beauchamp writes, *Sex-segregated bathrooms in the United States emerged roughly concurrently with the institutionalization of racially segregated bathrooms and other public spaces, as part of Jim Crow laws intensifying after the 1896 Plessy v. Ferguson decision. Because gendered bathrooms were constructed to alleviate the social upheaval provoked by white women's increased participation in public space,* Beauchamp continues, *these bathrooms actually protected the social hierarchy that designated the public arena as white men's domain. In this way, such spatial boundaries respond to and reinforce broader investments in the purity of not only individual bodies, but also social morals and national identity.* He concludes, in short, that *racially segregated public space is fading away though its fundamental remnants linger in more clearly marked gender divisions. This imagined decline of racial segregation suggests that the construction of racialized space informs current gendered divisions, with racial difference always present in gender difference.*[7]

Consider, finally, how black (~~cis~~?) women are often thought of as not-quite-women, not because black (~~cis~~?) women are undeserving of being seen as women or cannot measure up to the gendered category's implicit requisites of femininity—both of which are fraught sentiments—but because "woman" as a category of personhood is underlain by certain assumptions that are shaped by white femininity. For example, in 2007, Kadijah Farmer, a lesbian black woman who does not identify as transgender, was expelled from a bathroom at the Caliente Cab restaurant in New York. She was disallowed valid identification as "woman" by both a patron and a bouncer. Despite her cisgender identification, her blackness was presumed to disallow her from proper placement within womanhood. And she is not alone. Black women are subject to being "mules," as Zora Neale Hurston has said, when "women" are the "weaker" sex, fragile, passive; black women with children are reprimanded for not having jobs—and indeed are incessantly forced to get jobs and leave those children in others' hands when "women" must be good mothers and care for their children themselves; black women are disproportionately sterilized or deemed unfit for caring for their own children, when "women" are said to have motherhood as their highest calling.[8]

In a clear sense, writes Shaadi Devereaux,

> Black womanhood is inherently viewed as drag performance. . . . The assumption is always that Black women are all imitating "true women" with long silky hair, light eyes and a list of features not associated with Blackness. . . . We tend to overlook this in how we view what it means to be trans and cis (presenting in a way deemed normative to the gender you were assigned at birth) and who has access to narratives of womanhood.[9]

The unruly force that blackness entails causes gender and the untroubled grounds on which it gains its definitional categoricality to quake. It ain't about doing all the right things and staying properly on "this side" of perinatal gender assignations because sometimes one's very emergence into the world is a troubling relationship to the stability of sidedness. The blackness that some of us, via various avenues and roads and doors and windows, emerge into sociality through is the condition for deviation from the tenets of the gender binary. I want to understand this not merely as lamentable, as a violence to hopefully, someday, be remedied by inclusion into the cistem. I want to understand this, maybe, as a conditional possibility for a more just, capacious way to be gendered, to be ungendered, to be (trans)gendered in and out of the world.

Which is to say, the black and trans propelling my aims necessitate that I have beef with normativity, and gender normativity, the imposition of the exclusion of possibility as one's only possibility, is thrown into crisis with the insertion of blackness. This insertion, which is the insertion of a blackness of capacious figuration, generates some other kind of existence beyond what is proffered as the only possible arrangement for subjectivity. What is generated is something beyond mere representation, re-presentation of what has already been given, a givenness that possesses an originary violence. How might it be generative to think that those proximal to blackness's effects, a nonexclusionary and radically inclusive proximity, refuse to represent the thing—namely, cisgender—that they are demanded to represent? If blackness and those who engender their subjectivities through it cannot quite re-present cisgender but are forced to try to squeeze into it, what might be generative in the very fact that squeezing must occur in order to approximate a gender assignation that proclaims itself nonassignatory? I want to make the claim that it is not so simple to say that everyone who has not declared themselves transgender or genderqueer or nonbinary—shorthanded: noncis—is in fact cisgender, as there are those for whom the term does not fit who have made no such declaration, have made no corporeal interventions. To timidly offer a nonanalogous analogy so as not to mistakenly analogize race and gender as operating on the same axis (though that is also not to say that they do not travel asymptotically close to one another on similarly textured tracks): where *They*, a they not strictly referential of a demographic particularity but maybe a subjective indeterminacy, *wear the material they work like a bad habit, out of uniform(ity), between thread and protocol, seen and heard and danced as a kind of skin, a vehicle for passage, in and through the merely epidermal*, it might also be said that gender troubling, that the work of transing gender and (trans)gender, is to wear yet work a given materiality in and through and beyond the *merely [genital]*, the *merely [chromosomal]*. If the former rightly describes a different conception of blackness, the latter describes a different conception of transness, which is to say the trans as *ante normative persist[ence]* aerates and alternates away from a circumscriptive designation toward radical freedom.[10]

There is thus an inextricable relationship between blackness and transness requiring a constant entanglement between them manifesting as those who are, or who have become, or who are proximate to, or have emerged through blackness as never aligning, never matching gendered assignations, never "being" cis.

So when I think about that kid born in the middle of September in the early nineties, a kid who preferred action figures and video games and cartoons over bike-riding and parties and neighborhood games, I think about what I owe that kid. That little black boy who was not all the way a boy, a not all the wayness that proved an aperture into other worlds of body and relation, is owed something from me. There was a fear in that child; the preference for indoor mythicisms couched in imagined terrains and lifeworlds for action figures and the animated surrealities of cartoons was a desire to not have to deal with the curtailments of the outside. It is not to say that home was safe or without curtailment. That child knows too well the implicit and explicit demands to be a big boy, to stop crying, to stop bitching. Outside, too, had these demands, and from people much less loving than mom and grandma and big brother. This kid wanted to glimpse ways to move and think and express that did not have to yield to such hearty strictures.

To play with action figures—the Blue Power Ranger that kid had was a favorite—meant that these figures did not have to speak as others might have made them. They did not have to fight to the death, nor did they have to live on Earth. They did not have to even be "men." Blue Power Ranger could have looked like anything beneath that sleek suit, could have sounded like anything. And the best part: with a coalition of other colored and suited comrades who also did not have to look like or sound like particular categorical ways, Blue Power Ranger could morph—could mighty morph—into something else entirely. The mutability in this was alluring, so, so alluring. This is the kind of trans that this kid who was me, not all the way boy, felt in flits and flickers, an ineffable trans, right? Because that's what trans is, or might be, or ought to be—*there's something ineffable about transness that exceeds the terminological and the identitarian*, as Hil Malatino puts it, which permits his insistence on a hearty, hefty, trans *care*.[11] Yes, trans care, because I felt deeply cared for, like no other thing had done for me, by this alluring flickering trans.

**I wondered that though cisgender might indeed be who I am, maybe it isn't necessarily how I always feel, that maybe I can call myself queer in that I often identify as someone other than the person I appear to be. Though I am not trans, I might occasionally still be able to feel trans, partly because I had somewhere to change from, having started as cis in the first place.— Hilary Offman, "Queering of a Cisgender Psychoanalyst," 2017**

Trans becomes possible on the scene of intelligibility (to the extent that it can be said to be intelligible to the hegemon) through a departure from a stable gender: cisgender. But cisgender invokes stability only if we concede that the "match" between sex and gender is predicated on sex as firmly rooted and gender as having the possibility of straying from that fixed referent, and if such straying does not occur, one is cis. Yet we have, as feminists and queer theorists and trans theorists, committed to the assertion that sex, too, is not stable, not transparent, not fixed, thus the line blurs. Cis, then, and presumptions of its steadfast existence, its necessary existence, *reinscribes binary gender in the process of constituting its own intelligibility*, cis *makes the across (n.) that trans crosses over refer to the "line" between "male" and "female," as though we agree upon what and where that line may be as well as on what constitutes male and female*—which we profoundly do not.[12] So what are we even talking about? What are we vociferously insisting upon when we, me included, talk about the ravages, the privileges, the ignorances of cis folks?

The very notion of "alignment" or "matching," to be straight with y'all, is disingenuous. We know very well, and we've known this since, like, the nineties (my whole lifetime, basically), that the hard bifurcation between sex and gender is not quite right, for gender is not to the fabricated/fictive as sex is to the natural/real, and there is really no template for what role or corporeal configuration is supposed to "match" a sex assignation. The language of matching, integral to cisgender, has embedded within it a troubling assumption that there *is* a way to match one's given sex, which means that there *is* a right way to "be male/female," a statement that leaves a funky gender normative taste on one's tongue. The very structure of cisgender installs sex as a determinative propulsive force for how one ought to rightly behave as the sex they have been bestowed, or that they "are," meaning that sex comes decidedly before gender and dictates what gender will become. Decades of gender theory down the drain. Cisgender functions by way of stabilizing sex as the way to say that a variable gender aligns or does not align with a sex that is always and already in place, going nowhere and known in its entirety. Operating in this way with people wildin' out about the clear, obvious injustices toward transgender people as opposed, mutually exclusively, to cisgender people—though believe me, I get it and sympathize, truly—the rote distinction between cisgender and transgender does not attend to its messiness. The issue had here, and the issue for the cis/trans distinction I would say, is blackness.

In the mad black, mad radical corners of Twitter I see circulating, in a taking-seriously of those thinkers we genuflect to in all of our work in and outside of the academy, a steadfast assertion. It rubs folks the wrong way sometimes, whether in its simple declaration or in its sometimes (oftentimes?) failure to say more. In this corner with whom I might call, just a little inappropriately (but I'm from Philly so I get a little slack on this) "real nigga intellectuals," they say: "Black [the "B" is *always* capitalized] people can't be cisgender." The claim is backed by my intellectual loves, and I do not doubt that. And I can get down with it, I want to say, but I find myself, so very often, wanting more. I have an affective response, one characterized by an intellectual affinity but a visceral breath-holding, imperfectly manifesting simply as **Siiiiggggghhhh*, not this again* . . . But there is much more to say about this groan. This, here, is my saying more.

The issue of blackness for transness, then, writes Elías Cosenza Krell, seems to be that it uncovers the implicitly racist and classist underpinnings of hard-line categories of sex and gender.[13] That line is the line constituting cisness over which trans crosses, a line whose porosity and, frankly, perpetual motility is made plain by blackness's historical and contemporary effects. In short, blackness names the radicalization of gender in its anoriginal departure from the this-sidedness of cis.[14]

It's like, we *say*, as feminists and queer theorists and trans theorists, that we know the split between gender and sex is a constructed one, is bullshit, trash, to be banished with celerity; we *say* we do not believe in the immutability or naturalness or transparency of sex. But this seems to fall away when we claim to *know* that cis people have privileges that trans people do not. And, you know, we are right about that. And perhaps we ought to continue doing this. Or not. No, probably not. But I get it, I do. You see, the strong assertion of knowledge that there are cis people and there are noncis people—or, to put another thing down, flip it, and reverse it: that there are trans people and there are nontrans people—is a distinction that persists disingenuously and, moreover, because of racism: or, the installment of the racial as supplementary to the normative narrative of discerning who does and does not fall under the purview of modernity, which marks an aberrance that allows cisgender to congeal onto normative subjects, or whiteness, and gender deviance to adhere to racialized or blackened subjects.

So maybe it's not quite "Black people can't be cisgender." It is, rather, that blackness undermines the embedded coherency, transparency, and immutability of cisgender. Cisgender, when approaching my blackness, tries to tell me its stiches fit my torso but ends up too snug in some places, too loose in others, and missing entire sections, buttons and zippers, pockets and in-seams. It is thought because I have been given this garment, or, more acutely, this skin, this set of genitals, this musculature, that the way they have been read on others is how they should be read on me. I have long thought so, too, wanting to attend to the violence I might portend or privileges I might accrue. But maybe, because of my blackness, and maybe all of you who might be proximate to blackness inasmuch as *everyone whom blackness claims, which is to say everyone, can claim blackness*, can feel otherwise than the cisness you got dealt.[15] Maybe you, we, can understand ourselves through a certain kind of noncisness, a certain kind of transness, in that we, like Offman in the epigraph above, "often identify as someone other than the person I appear to be." And blackness can make a mirage of appearance, dissembling on a dime and nickel and penny. We have not been gifted other, more legible attributes of trans, but maybe we, if we commit to what the term demands of us, "might occasionally still be able to feel trans, partly because I had somewhere to change from, having started as cis in the first place"—or even if we never started as cis at all.

A THOUGHT BY my friend and comrade, my black trans homie, Marshall Green, who loves black people and blackness, loves trans people and transness, loves their imbrications, and loves to think, to do, radical abolitionist thought as a precursor to and articulation of love.

> An androgynous self is not easily recognizable within the confines of our knowledge, which insist that *the human* be predicated first on the recognition of either woman or man, and anything other than that becomes deviant and dehumanized. We can also only see these subjects if they are in motion toward becoming either man or woman. To occupy this liminal space without the desire to become or to be something legible to the world as either male or female is a radical stance, proving that there are other ways of being. This is at the heart of an androgynous politic, which, like *the Black woman,* is situated in the margins of the margins, not asking to be let in to frameworks of either/or, but instead insisting upon an interrogation of how this binary thinking has a way of policing and oppressing rather than building strong collectives and coalitions. A Black feminist stance is an androgynous stance that refuses to choose one thing over another as it already knows that game to be a farce, which does more to distort problems than to illuminate them in their full complexity. An androgynous politic or modality is one that is able to occupy the marginal spaces, not in hopes of someday penetrating the *normal,* but instead always working through and toward possibilities outside of those

that have been deemed permissible by the state. There is indeed *something else* to be, and there is much difficulty in the practice of deciphering that something else to be on its own terms—what are the tools necessary for seeing differently something different?

Trans* is a tool. . . .[16]

What Green is calling an androgynous politic is not, I believe, an argument for the purported salvific effects of having the look of someone exactly in between "man" and "woman," as if such a discernible look is readily known to us or has any kind of substantive political weight. What Green seems to be suggesting via the radicality of black feminism, a trans feminist blackness, is a politic they are calling androgynous precisely because it exceeds the dictates and grammars of the gender binary. Androgyny, as an analytic referent to be mobilized politically, is neither man nor woman and is, in some ways, both man and woman, fracturing at once the mutual exclusivity of man and woman as well as the requirement to be *either* man or woman. The confines of our knowledge are structured on a gender binaristic framework whose architecture does not permit different materials or blueprints. Androgynous politics might be a name for the politics that emerge from recognition of the disjuncture between blackness and cisgender, creating a manner of livability and doing life that thrusts forth from the politicized desire for Green's *something else to be.* If being human insists that one must be man or woman, political androgyny—which is to say, in my language, cistem failure, the enactment of a failed cistem—undoes what the human is and works toward creating something new in its wake. It claims the monstrosity of the deviant and dehumanized as the place from which another gendered mode, another non- and ungendered mode, of life begins.

Those subjects seen by virtue of their being in motion toward becoming man or woman make us wary and make all the more enticing the gifts of dissemblance and ocular evasion blackness bestows, and the gifts of corporeal confoundment and sex/gender-locus shell-gaming that trans—or (trans)gender—bestows. How to love and make space for the "radical stance" of not being the man, the woman demanded of you even if or when your body registers to them only on grounds of presumed alignment? How to enact in infinite ways the disjuncture you feel and profess in realms not simply attached to the normative confines of "the body"? Generating life on and from the margin of the margins, where the margins do not have to constitute the inside but can exist apart from it, valid on its own terms, doing things differently over there in the dark, in the uncomfortable, in the afterlife and afterparty where race and gender no longer hold but where *blackness* and *transness*, *blackness* and *(trans)gender* still do it up like a love supreme because that's what they are—supreme kinds of love for the transitivity, for the anoriginal, for the lawless, for the anarchic ectopic womb. This is where the pursuit is not of assimilation or the marketed joys of *this*; this is where the pursuit is for possibilities not known or legible, for a whole new game where your controllers and guidebooks and cords and buttons do not, cannot, work.

I WAS SITTING at a table on the patio of a lovely little restaurant in Dartmouth with a colleague and our new friend. During our walk I shared a bit about the writing that I do, said that my intellectual pursuits revolved primarily around blackness, trans studies, and feminism. It was made clear that my political commitments were focused on gender nonnormativity, and the ease with which I used *trans* and *they* pronouns and the language endemic to queer and trans cultural productions attested to a certain level of dexterity with the topic.

Our new friend, as we sat, shared her own scholarly pursuits, those of Asian American literature and cultural studies. Somehow, and I truly don't remember how, my colleague (a white woman who brilliantly writes about Indigenous and African American speculative fictions) noted how she and I have had numerous conversations about the ethics and navigational attention of those like us who are presumed "outside" of the implicit demographics of the disciplines we take part in. "Wait," our new friend said, "you're not trans?"

This, or something like this, has happened to me over a dozen times now (and counting). Being invited to give my "personal" story on "black trans identity" or asked to participate on "all trans" panels leaves me with a deeply vexed feeling. And once I had a grad student tell me that *mad people assume you're a trans man*. Most times I want to say all I've said up to this point. But oftentimes I cower and capitulate, unable to fully say what it is I must say to stop the assumptions from occurring. Unable to say, in not so many words: yes, but no; not the kind of trans you likely think, which is likely the only trans you think there is—there is another way, are other ways, to do and be trans. And I roam there.

I'm vexed because these assumptions are neither true nor false. It would be ethically suspect for me to just go along with the thinking that I'm trans, as I do not and have not had the experiences commonly attributed to transgender people: undergoing medical and psychological scrutiny and surveillance, having legislation passed to invalidate my (gendered) existence, encountering violence and its various specters on the street because my voice or my body or my gait does not "match" assessed gendered cues. These are not experiences I can claim as my own, wholly—experiences that very often go under the banner of "being transgender." And yet I so badly want to live an intellectually rigorous and constituent life. I want to take seriously the words of the thinkers and activists I so dearly respect, many of whom grace this essay. They have edified me, maybe even corrupted me, to think in a way that expands the capacity of "trans" to hold so much more than it is believed to be able to hold. I want to stand firm, courageously, in the thinking of the prefixal trans, the trans that has the capacity to mean not only those who have undergone the aforementioned experiences but also those who deploy their (un)gendered embodiment, (un)gendered intellectual apparatuses, and (un)gendered politics in ways that do the work of transing—a *practice that takes place within, as well as across or between, gendered spaces*, a practice that fucks with gender and disassembles/reassembles what gender and subjectivity can mean; trans as a mode of analysis rather than a (mere) identity category.[17] What would *that* entail? What kind of rethinking would we have to undergo if that were taken brutally, terrifyingly seriously?

What would it entail if one were to submit as veracious that *trans* and maybe even *transgender* are not so much identificatory categorizations demanding strict adherence to only a specific set of bodily characteristics but *modes of critique*, or more interestingly *modes of analysis*, to take on the language of Toby Beauchamp? Many of us say this is what we mean, but when it comes to following through we gasp at the audacity of those of us who are actually grappling with how it might force the discomfort of those who presumed themselves past the uncomfortable part. People of trans experience or people who have been assigned one gender perinatally and depart from it via surgical, hormonal, or sartorial means are certainly still part of this endeavor, so do not misread my intellectual dwellings as depriving them of valid proximity to transness. This is to expand an already expansive signifier for radical work, a taking to task of those who do not wish to do that work and have it impact their livelihood.

Gender has been lodged in the epistemic position of sexual indexicality, or basically: it's thought of as the nice word for talking about genitals and (biological) sex. Thou shan't say *sex* or *genitalia* in polite company. What trans as a methodological, analytical critique does is put the squeeze on the very idea of gender *merely as a social, linguistic, or subjective representation of an objectively knowable material sex.*[18] Sloughing off the haughtiness embedded in knowing another's sex by purportedly knowing another's gender, (trans)gender marks a phrasal reckoning with the fuzziness and ultimate inaccessibility of the teleological one-to-one relationship between what is called *sex* and what is called *gender*. *And* this matter, for me, at the level of the viscerally personal, circulates with a notion of blackness that *is* the "mode of critique" given in the trans, which presents an astounding site for dwelling: more than even asking if my epidermalized blackness troubles the coherence on which cisgender rests, I want to ask how the noncis space blackness implies and the noncis space transness more readily names might entangle themselves to the point of making necessary the proclamation that blackness rhymes with transness.

I promise it is not for selfish reasons I want to usher in this reevaluation of (trans)gender. And I hope I come off as genuine, as someone who wishes only to make life more livable for those who fall on the outside of our world order. I hope this, but know I may very well fail in the eyes of some of you, and I cannot blame you. You mean well and you are trying only, I believe, to make sure that more folks do not meet their graves too soon.

: : :

Yet at the scene of addressability the call can fall flat, as it does for me often with *he* and *man*. There is a wonder about how one is to navigate the failure of address, not when the address is one cast, primarily, as demeaning or purposely contrary to one's voiced wishes as in willfully misgendering a trans woman, for example. What I am curious about is the failure of address when one is presumably the proper subject of the address and there is no malice in the address; indeed, the address is understood as mere description. The address that has me in its sights delivers to me, and seeks to engender me through, en*gender* me through, various iterations of *he*. And it lands, I turn at the call, implicating myself. Most times. But sometimes I do not turn, and sometimes I turn at other names.

Yes, yes, I know, pronouns are important not only as respectful ways of encountering someone on nonviolent grounds but also as indices for social positioning. It is the latter that preoccupies me. Yes, I turn at the *he*, but at times I do not turn, and at times I turn—when it is offered, blessedly—at the *they*, and this all matters. And sometimes I just ghostride the whip, with my body showing up but no one there to affirm or deny its coding, a refusal of the cisness it demands that I even acknowledge. The nature, though, of the commingling converges on how gender operates around my subjectivity, and how my blackness, as somatic endowment and paraontological affinity, necessarily disturbs the subtending coherency of gender as such, does not make for proper cisgender alignment. Even when turning at the *he*, I submit, it cannot be held that I am cis. Neither revoking boringly termed privileges nor the violence my perceived alignment portends, I aim to cultivate a space of (trans)gender that serves as a ground where those who misalign despite their given cisness can operate in their beings. And they operate via their misinterpellation. Their hailings, our hailing, with seemingly appropriate *he*s and *she*s are inadequate, and always inadequate irrespective of the belief by others that the hailings land comfortably. We turn sometimes even though the interpellations are wrong, are always wrong because they render us evacuated of the other deeply substantive ways wherein cisness is loosened or vitiated. Within our subjectivity is not simply the body that is made to house an unwelcomed alignment but so much more, a *multiplicity and anarchic complexity* that is obscured by a "cis" that renders us *manifestly unknowable by projecting onto [us] a single unitary self that, being false, offers nothing to "know" at all.*[19] How can I say that even if you smirk at your success at having "properly" gendered me simply because I turned, there has still been no knowledge gained? How can I say that cis, even if presumed to have landed, disintegrates at the point of contact and explodes in other realms of subjective life, discursive, interpersonal, sociopolitical, intellectual realms?

*I've got nothing left to give to the gender binary, even though I might get kissed in its shadow.*[20]

Harnessing this *mis*interpellation presents precisely the (trans)gender space where I might hope to be actualized, or at least caressed and nurtured on my way to a nondestinational gendered nega-destination, if you will. Not properly "transgender," the criteria for which is always nebulous and purposely fuzzy so as not to fix its indexical unfixing, and not properly cisgender, where I can come alive—in many ways quite literally—is in the (trans)gender as emergent subjectivity, however blurry and inchoate. It is a commitment by those who are mis/interpellated as cis to repudiate cisness and reject its sole province as confined to the legible body—that is, a repudiation of cisgender as solely and primarily the province of the legible body. (Trans)gender can be the kind of space hospitable to black "cis" subjects, "cis" subjects whose ultrabody articulations are thoroughly, seethingly trans. It becomes the kind of space committed to not replicating the norms that got us in this mess in the first place, for that is what those who demand, unceasingly, that we be cis are unwittingly encouraging, the perpetuation of cisness. But that is not the end goal, it cannot be, though I know deeply how much there needs to be acknowledgement of privileges bestowed on those who turn when the call is levied. The present condition nevertheless is primped and groomed by those being cis; it is their (maybe I should say "our," though I do not wish to and hope it is OK with you, reader, if I do not) doing that has created the conditions for transantagonism and the valorization of cisnormativity.

WHAT I AM TRYING to offer is perhaps a different way to think about how we subjectivate ourselves, and in particular how we find coalitional affiliation, how we find kinfolk, based primarily on those otherwise modes of subjectivation. I am urged by the solicitation of a (trans)gender space the subject of these notes to refuse to allow one's putatively immutable and transparent identity to be the end of how they can emerge into relation with others or articulate the parameters of the world; rather, the efficacy that erupts from one's doing of their gender in bad ways, those who kick cisness to the curb even if others constantly bring it back to one's doorstep is affixed to a subjective, which is to say discursive and relational and intellectual and sociopolitical, aberrance. The relocation of where cisness and transness might lie is what I am most interested in. I want to sashay, if you will, toward locating transness, a particular kind of transness to be found in the noncis/nontransgender space of (trans)gender, in excess of determined criteria of physiognomy, in excess of the visually legible, and more in movement in subversion of hegemonic power via various identity vectors.

Ugh, I feel a little icky saying all this right now. I feel appropriative and out of my lane. I feel *wrong*. But that wrong feeling is not "wrong" so much as it is, if I'm trying to be kind to myself, misaligned with current dogma. I'm making a break for it away from normative sociodiscursive entrapments that prohibit certain things to be said and thought. But I'm making a break only because that is the abolitionist strain in the trans as I understand it: to break from regulative constraints, constraints thought to be impenetrable and deemed blasphemous if broken from. I don't want to paint myself as an intellectual martyr doing the bold work few dare to do. That's not it. That's not it at all. But y'all might feel like that's it. Hence my ickiness.

But there was this thing Riki Wilchins said that I keep returning to. The proprietary relationship some trans folks have to strict parameters around qualification for trans status presumes an inherency to trans being. It presumes that one is trans only when criteria are met, criteria pertaining to some perceived inherent meaning to a certain kind of (altered) body. But, Wilchins says, *meanings do not cling to bodies like some kind of glutinous vapor or semiotic paste.* Meanings are never fixed in place, so the meaning of transness, too, more so than other meanings maybe, is not only never fixed but names never-fixity. It names, maybe, the refusal of being named, as naming is a power-hungry inaugurative practice to engender us from without, ahead of ourselves, in service of another's agenda—*every meaning attaching to our bodies was put there by someone, long ago. Every gendered scar on my psyche has distinctly non-transexual fingerprints, and they show up with the lightest dusting and in the poorest light.*[21] And this process—which is gender itself, always the ascriptive and prescriptive—occurs in tiny movements and pushes. Move this way, don't move that way, do this, don't do that, be this and don't be that or there will be hell to pay. The trans that Wilchins advances is a subjectless critique. It is a trans unattached to a specific kind of body and placed in a dispositional force of unfitting. That unfitting is toned and textured in mutinous ways and supervenes on no linear line.

This trans is inviting, nonexclusionary, fed up with criteria for bodily inclusion because what even is a body but a placed enclosure on an unruly assemblage of parts that mean and remean and unmean all the time? Trans, then, is not an identity but an openness to identity's discontents, its undermining and subversion, its proliferation and, in the end, abolition. *The doors of identity must always remain open*, never closed so as not to foreclose another way we can get outside of the hellish landscape regulated by cisnormativity—the requisite to stay, always and forever, on the side they dictated for you.[22]

And all this from one of those deeply activistic on-the-ground trans people. I promise I am not trying to make the thinking housed in the academic filigree of university presses and endowed chairs and pedigreed departments hold sway. This thinking comes from other places and seeps into other places; the walls of the academy, when it comes to transness, crumble. I'm getting all of this stuff from the person who was out there when the Michigan Womyn's Festival was doing its trans-antagonistic thing and said, Nah, raincheck this wack show of solidarity through transantagonism. We goin' across the road and doing our own thing. This is an orientation toward and away from orientations that hinder and clamp down on modes of livable life. This is a disorientation *as* an orientation. Which might describe Wilchins's *Transexual Menace*. (Wilchins preferring the single *-s* transexual instead of the more pervasive double *-ss*.)

I so badly wanted to be down with the Menaces, but, when reading about this gloriously transradical collective, didn't think I was allowed. I just knew that one had to be transsexual to be a Menace; I just knew that my desire to be part of the collective was just another cis-adjacent effort of colonization and appropriation. I just knew it. But that couldn't be it. This way of thinking feels too radical to lap up staid, rote rules for exclusion, I thought to myself. And I think this is very much the case. *First of all, you don't have to be transexual to be a Menace*, Wilchins says.

*Anyone can be a member. It's more of a disorganization than anything else.* And this is not a move of absolution or cis capitulation. Do not write it off as such. I wanted to, and want to, take this seriously—if anyone can be a Menace, what does that make the designation "transexual menace"? It makes it, I think, categorically irreverent, and one comes into Menaceness to the extent to which one irreveres the categorical imperative, to the extent to which one refuses transantagonism, not the extent to which one "is" transsexual. To be a Menace is to menace, from the Latin *minae:* to threaten. To be a Menace is to threaten the order, to threaten organization, to be a menace to the binary, whether you look like this or that; it is about how you menace the regulative regimes that say you must look like this or that. Those regimes demand so many contortions into nonchosen categories, and that is the issue here. So, since *even such "hard" categories as gender, race, sex, and orientation are not causes of our oppression but its effects*, we need *a new kind of political struggle, one that seeks not just to overthrow the oppression, but the categories as well.* We need *a movement without identities*, Wilchins says.[23] We need abolition. That is what trans moves toward.

This blasphemous meditation that might, to some, howl as an abnegation of the privileging effects of my status as read as, but not, cisgender is actually, for me, I hope, a commitment to other forms of livability that reject wholeheartedly the tenets of this world. It is the project of abolition, an abolition that cannot hold on to some parts of the world that make us more comfortable, especially when we hold on to them only because they are all we've ever known even though we know, we *know*, they are harmful and deleterious hang-ups. On the way to abolition it may very well be justifiable that we hold on to some of our violent categorizations, but at what point are you committed to relinquishing them if we cannot achieve abolition—if abolition is even an achievable goal that we once and for all arrive at—until we relinquish them? We must relinquish in order to begin to actualize abolition, yet you will not relinquish until abolition is achieved. You see my frustration.

We continue, understandably, to venerate the twinkling twilight of those old idols any Nietzschean might reveal is a misstep, though those idols have long served as a hearty place of sense-making. Those idols cannot serve us ad infinitum; they stifle us, are unable to give what we need in this time, now, here. I am imagining, then, the dawn of not even new idols but the eradication of idolatry.

# BLOWING UP NARNIA

A 1998 British Broadcasting Channel production. Text appears on the screen: London 1940. The four children walk up to their home on break from school for the holidays, greeted by the prim and proper Mrs. Macready, wizened hair and gray (or *grey*; this is, after all, the UK) suit, standing regal, bespectacled. The children leave their bags just beyond the entrance and are told that the servants will take them. "That is their function," Mrs. Macready says. "One must not be deprived of their function. Everyone has their part to play." I think: there are some whose function is one that disallows others' functioning, some whose function is cast outward toward disabling others' flourishing. The part some have to play, a part they decided for themselves and a part that, like bossy children wanting the biggest slice of cake, puts them at the pinnacle of the social order, is a part that might cause trepidation. And fear. And harm. What happens when your part is frightening to you, a part given to you that you do not want, a part that others who have had your part demand you represent flawlessly or you get kicked out of the performance for good, a part that is not only frightening but does not fit you, a part that you have grown out of or never fit to begin with or know fits no one and makes others deeply, deeply uncomfortable, unable to play their parts, unable to act anymore, unable?

The patriarch comes into the room. The Professor. He instructs the servants to bring the children's meals to their rooms, for they do not wish to converse with an old man upon their arrival. Mrs. Macready disagrees, thinking it improper to dine in one's sleeping quarters. All things must have their proper place, I suppose. The Professor puts his foot down. "Whatever you say, Professor. Your word is law," she responds, demurely. And law it is, Professor. Your word, as patriarch, is quite literally law, a discursive and juridical mandate emerging from patriarchal power codified over eras of, indeed, the discursive and juridical mandate that has emerged from you.

The children get settled and play hide-and-seek. Lucy, the youngest girl, hides in an old wardrobe. Rummaging past old sweaters, she finds herself in a mythical land, covered in snow, and she meets Mr. Tumnus, a pleasant faun. He is baffled as to why a human girl would be in Narnia, asking if she is the "daughter of Eve." They chat. Lucy worries about getting back to her siblings to tell them of the wondrous time she had in this new land. Upon sharing the news with them, however, they do not believe her. "Why don't you admit it was all a story?" Susan asks. Lucy is disheartened, so she tries to show them, only to enter the wardrobe and meet its back—hard wood and far from a vast land of snow and mythical creatures. Admit it was all a story.

But the disbelief does not last long, as Edmund, the younger brother, finds his way into Narnia, unbeknownst to him. He tries to call out for his sister in order to apologize, to share in a mutual delight, but she is not there. His calls in Narnia go unanswered, so of course it is "just like a girl. Sulking. Won't accept a fellow's apology."

He is met by the White Witch, who is initially peeved at his ignorance as to who she is, but, once finding out that he is a human, a "son of Adam" (because apparently one is only the child of the parent of the "same" gender; one is never the son of Eve or daughter of Adam), she instructs him to fetch his siblings, lure them into Narnia, so he, on her promise, can become king. He does just that, though such is only the beginning of the story.

Narnia has long intrigued me, ever since I first read C. S. Lewis's *The Chronicles of Narnia: The Lion, the Witch, and the Wardrobe* in sixth grade. It was the first book I had read cover to cover, and I was enchanted. As I understand it, Narnia is a magical place where only a privileged few are granted access. To gain entry, one must in fact disallow critical knowledge: that it exists, that it is a world among other possible worlds. Its entry depends on an epistemological ignorance of the very possibility of worlds outside of its confines, the complexity and existence and texture of the space and people who are not permitted inside—or the people who have gone off to live in ways that do not attest to Narnia's singularity. One must also, as the White Witch implies, hold this other world outside of Narnia in contempt, as it poses an imminent threat to Narnia's existence. When apprised of Edmund's point of entry into Narnia, she is overcome with fright: "This may wreck all," she gasps. Non-Narnia's knowledge of Narnia could wreck it, not only because Non-Narnia might breach Narnia and fundamentally alter it, but also because Narnia would then be forced to seriously grapple with how they do things in Non-Narnia. With how Narnia might *deserve* the threat.

Narnia touts itself as on the right side, indeed the only side.

**They bust open the wardrobe to a Narnia of worlds that The Cisgenders have monopolized for far too long.—Sessi Kuwabara Blanchard, "In Defense of the Trans Villainess," 2018**

Narnia. It is a land constituted by an orchestrated construction it must obscure in order to tout itself as natural. Its hierarchies must remain divinely ordained; its citizens must be in the places proper to them, bestowed by a law out of anyone's control. Narnia, it thinks, is detached from the fanciful flights characterizing those not under its fold—indeed, does not even consider others as possessing the capacity for knowledge, for reality, for legitimate existence. Narnia does the cartographical point-plotting; Narnia decides what counts as a body, what counts as the locus of bodily legitimacy, what counts as a problem to that legitimacy, a solution, here, there, nowhere. Narnia, in all its haughtiness, possesses the hubris of an origin: that all that exists refers to, learns from, is valued in light of it. But Narnia is no longer, and never really was, tenable. It, like the hubristic requisite of alignment, of remaining on and asserting valid knowledge only from and as this side, of *cisness*—my analogic connection to Narnia, as they are bound together in texture and rhetoric, in purpose and presumption—thinks itself the only vantage from which to encounter life. From which, indeed, to emerge into life. All reality begins from it, and in this beginningness (the arrogant assumption of a kind of divinity, as the biblical *In the beginning, God* . . . echoes resoundingly here) it disallows other beginnings. No other vantage can hold sway; indeed, there are no other vantages.

What I wish for deeply is something we don't have yet that might emerge from a failure to inherit the lineage bestowed upon us. That which might emerge if we manage to cultivate a conditional refusal of cis alignment and the violences therein, the thing that emerges when its condition of possibility is a constant refusal of what has come to be coercively demanded of us. The question that presents itself to us, in this initial moment, is why? Why do such a thing, why fail to inherit what we are told is our birthright, why give up that which gives us over to the world as the powerful, competent beasts we quite vigorously want to be, be, be?

What is gained from this failure is another kind of life to be lived that does not require a constant murder of emergent subjectivities that do not fit. Too, what is gained is a different groove for us to trek along and to step to, a groove that references a relation between us on grounds more hospitable, loving, open, vulnerable, proliferative. To fail at our inheritance is to spit in our ancestors' faces, and I want the spit to be venomous. There is much talk, albeit from a different kind of lineage, about venerating our ancestors, acknowledging how those before us have enabled our life. And I love those ancestors. We have, though, a hefty genealogy of ancestors, as some of them are the drunk uncle who fucked up the planet for us, the shady cousin who gave us nudie magazines in our youth, the violent brother who used to hit us when mom's back was turned, the stepdad who told us that no one would ever, ever love us if we did not dominate, did not win, did not kill, did not devour the lot of weaklings in our path. Those ancestors cannot continue to hold sway in how our world unfolds. They cannot be forgotten, I know; they cannot be disowned as if they did not place their grubby hands on the soil on which we try to walk. They can, though, be *disavowed*: declared invalid, recalled, refused to be associated with. They have given us something they felt sacred. Some of it we do not want, and dare not retain, for what they've given us is deadly.

Inasmuch as I have been given this side as my own birthright and have been understood as having not given that up, I am uniquely called to task. What I have been called to task on is how I take my own strides, how my own subjectivity bears on my thinking. It is often an indictment, one I need, one that refuses to let me off the hook. Are you, they ask, blowing up your Narnia? Far from simply saying *Yes*, digging my heels into my self-identification as a feminist—a weak-ass move if there ever was one, using identificatory proclamation in lieu of putting in the radical work of undoing one's subjectivity and agitating, via myriad means, for sociopolitical devastation—what I am indicted for is any trace of enjoying the fruits of what is often shallowly called privilege garnered by how my gender is read. What I am tasked with, then, is an unbecoming. That unbecoming is being called another name, a name that I timidly find myself enlivened by. In some circles the name is *queer*, in others *trans*. But sometimes I cannot lay claim to these names. And, some other times, they are the only names I ever want to call myself even if no one has ever called me them.

REMEMBER WHEN VINES were a thing? Short clips of often humorous and instantly quotable occurrences in everyday people's lives. I've grown to appreciate them more as I've gotten older, having on multiple occasions fallen down a YouTube rabbit hole of Vine after Vine. There is one that always gets me. A child in a field saturated with the squawks of moderately sized white birds. We call these birds "geese." The camera scans the field's avian serenity and lands on the child's face, staring intently at the birds, then up to the sky at the flying birds we also call geese. But the child does not call these birds geese. "Look over there, look over there," the child tells the person holding the camera. And then, with a flourish of the hand, the child says it, the phrase that went viral.

*Look at all those chickens!*

The kicker is that the birds were not chickens; they were geese. But the child was so sure, so confident that they were chickens. And perhaps the child, who could have been no more than five, was not "mistaken" per se but had only one word for winged, feathery, flying creatures: chickens. When you have inadequate language for a phenomenon you rely on what you have, paltry as it may be. If unchecked, you might become adamant, maybe even violent, about there being only chickens. There are no other birds. I've been calling them chickens my whole life. What are *geese*?

Paltry language is not merely a shoulder-shrugging "Oh, well, this is all we have"; linguistic scarcity is emplotted. We have no language for something oftentimes because the existing language claims that it is the only language there could and should be. Language, as Barthes would have it, is fascistic. To be possible in the world is, in some ways, to be given language through which to emerge. I know who you are because I know what to call you, and thus the rules and regulations for relating to you. I call you *chicken*, because that is the name for someone like you, and there are no other names for someone like you. And even if you look a bit off, like a weird chicken, all there are are chickens, so you are not a *goose* but a defective chicken. Which means you are a wrong chicken, not a right goose. The language and names at hand amount to *coercive laws*, Barthes writes, laws that *permit communication . . . but in exchange (or on the other hand) impose a way of being, a subjecthood, a subjectivity on one: under the weight of syntax, one must be this very subject and not another.*[1] Be a chicken, or else. If I see "geese," which are not a thing, I will exterminate them. Because geese will threaten the existence of chickens, which are all there are. Be chickens because you can be nothing else. Or, be chickens or I will make sure that you can be nothing else.

What happens when we (think we) only have two words for what people, and nonhuman animals, are? We encounter human geese but so quickly, so confidently, call them chickens, and maybe hens. And that is all. You aren't a chicken? Then what *are* you? You are a winged, feathery, flying creature, therefore you are a chicken. There are no other kinds of birds. Just chickens. *Goose* is made up, a defiance in the face of nature. My taxonomy is natural law; here in Narnia we only have lions and witches and fauns. *Humans*? Mythical.

And yet humans there are.

**Identity failed me. . . . I have been traversing the sunless territory of non-identity.—Virginia Woolf, *The Waves*, 1931**

Cistem failure does not have an identifiable look. I mean, one cannot read on another the failure of the cistem, as such would in fact undermine the aim, partly: that one cannot make recourse to the identifiable body as revealing, transparently, the gender or nongender of that body. The blowing up of Narnia and its attending cisnormative assumptions—that all bodies are and will only ever be cis, the transing of bodies and surgical interventions confirming gender subjectivity mere ruses papering over immutable hardware—results in the radical fracturing of how we come to mean in relation to one another. It opens up another possible world. Where I want to go is someplace else, ambling about in the remains of *cut up men* through a shadowy radical feminism enthralled with *murky modes of undoing, unbecoming, and violating.*[2] Where I want to go is the place where identity fails and we traverse Woolf's sunless territory of non-identity because that right there, with its non-ness, its un-ness, is the start of blowing stuff up in the magical land of Narnia.

Having no identity, things then get epically, beautifully, generatively weird. Dionne Brand said something once that messed me up, gloriously:

> And then there was one, another woman who did not want to be in the world, or the world she was dragged into, who noticed right away the fatal harm but who gave birth to a woman who wanted to be in the world true and absolutely whole and therefore lived with ghosts since that world could not happen yet. . . . These two women even when they gave birth to men the men were women. That is. They were undone by something or other and lay on apartment floors gurgling up some exhaustion with masculinity or killed that exhaustion in some violent Greyhound flight from Miami to New York.[3]

The woman of whom she speaks is a woman who might not be a woman, "woman" being the closest approximation to that minoritarian force implicatory of an evacuation of racialized gendered normativity. This woman, no doubt for Brand a woman colliding with blackness, does not wish to be in the world because the world cannot hold her. She was thrown, dragged into the world when she did not and could not inhabit the world on terms of her own precisely because those terms would render the destruction of the world. Those terms are unworldly terms. She is "she," she is a "woman," only because those are what the world has given to her, but she is more eruptive than that, and if that subjective eruption were to be permitted she would not be a being in this world. Those are what she was given in order to inhabit, and to be allowed to remain uncritiqued in, the Narnia into which she was thrown, dragged. Narnia demanded either he or she. The ghosts the woman birthed by the other woman were haunted by are specters of worlds outside of Narnia. They bespeak a world that has not yet happened because Narnia has stanched its actualization, for Narnia does not wish its own demise. The ghosts were futuristic traces of the ash of Narnia. And those ghosts were surely present when the women gave birth to men who were also women, because those men were surely black and could not be, did not wish to be, the kinds of men the world demanded they be. So, they were women, expressions of a kind of detonated first tier of Narnia, with innumerable tiers to go, but at least one is down. These men who were women strike me as illustrious possibilities, maybe even kin to me, my siblings, as maybe, if I could count myself worthy enough, we all came from the same womb. These men who were women gurgled up their exhaustion with cis masculinity, as I try to do; they came into the world via that exhaustion, as I hope to do. They live at the precipice of the end of Narnia's reign.

The aim is not just for men to "become" women. (I think "women" should also be in quotes. . . .) I do not want to become a woman; that, to me, is not what gendered liberation looks like, nor is it what must occur for me to "be" trans. "Woman," categorically, is also a violence. Not of the same register and tenor of "man," sure, but a violence nonetheless. In my younger years, when I, naïvely, thought to myself that maybe life would be better as not a girl, but, *not a boy*, I was reaching for something else. But maybe all I had then was a hope that "the other" gender would not constrict my airways as much, or would constrict them differently, a difference that would be welcomed if only because it might tap other pathways that might feel gentler. But now, in not wanting to be a man, not wanting to bound about the world launching masculinity's archive ahead of me, I neither want to be a woman nor to proliferate, necessarily, femininity. I am certainly, by most metrics, not feminine. (Perhaps the issue is with metrics themselves?) At least not corporeally or sartorially. Though I suspect there might be a realm in which femininity treads that is not simply about the visual, a realm inclusive of other modalities of relation. But that's the thing: Why must I *be* a gender? Must I be woman, feminine, if not man, masculine? If I assert another posture for my body and extra-/nonbody, will it inevitably be inducted into the closest category we have? It feels like I am in pursuit of becoming something else entirely by seeking, first, now, to be nobody. And that requires no spectacular alteration, it requires no passing of a threshold in order to enter into valid unterrain. I wish not to be anybody, really, for to be somebody is subject to the extant registers that cannot hold breadth. While being nobody—not yet a blown up somebody but perhaps a somebody with ticking timebombs strapped to it, impending doom lived ebulliently—I'm chillin' with ghosts and specters who, too, are nobodies, having no gender because they never lived and were not subject to this world's grammars, and thus never really died either.[4] I would like some other kind of being, ungendered or nongendered or too enthralled with something else there is no time to consider gender. And I would like to not have to die to get there. Or maybe I *must* die to get there. And then I'll finally be able to live.

THE CONFLAGRATORY LANGUAGE I use to denote the dismantling of cis genders might belie my intentions, both that of how cisness happens via accrual as well as that of how blowing things up can be read along masculinist lines. I am sorry for this, I am. And I hope such a slippage is permitted if only because, as I see it, the demise of the gargantuan citadel that is alignment with the gender binary is helpfully understood in language that evokes the spectacular. But, really, it is a tiny, quotidian accrual that makes cis genders so inviolable. It happens and happens, in small gestures and moments, in quiet and timid events. Almost imperceptible at times, natural and normal at other times. This is how it works so well. If we don't notice something is happening we cannot say that something has happened, only that this is how it is, nothing happened, in fact, it just is, was, and always will be. Such is its strength, its longevity. How sneaky it is, creeping along the sides of walls.

It happens when we are deemed *he*, forced to carry all that *he* entails—trucks to haul our huge loads, muscles to ensure that no one fucks with us, and of course guns to keep all the outside agitators at bay. This little tiny *he* is made to wear appropriate clothing, both in form and content: never a dress, never pink; always scrawled onto which is something like

"Lock Up Your Daughters" since *he* is most definitely out to rapaciously sexually consume all the women out there because that is how he becomes more *he* than all the other *he*s. Perhaps *he* never had a chance, too unaware and young to know what was happening. Perhaps there is nothing to be done now that the damage is already dealt. But perhaps, too, now is the only time something *can* be done, and to do nothing now is the truly damaging act.

It happens when we *know* that there are clear ways to "be" a girl, and dead giveaways when boys try, but fail, to be *real* girls. Someone like Huckleberry Finn found this out the hard way. *Bless you, child*, the woman in St. Petersburg told Huck when it became clear to her that he wasn't the Sarah Williams or the Mary Williams he first (and then second) said he was. *When you set out to thread a needle don't hold the thread still and fetch the needle up to it; hold the needle still and poke the thread at it; that's the way a woman most always does, but a man always does t'other way. And when you throw at a rat or anything, hitch yourself up a tiptoe and fetch your hand up over your head as awkward as you can, and miss your rat about six or seven foot. Throw stiff-armed from the shoulder, like there was a pivot there for it to turn on, like a girl; not from the wrist and elbow, with your arm out to one side, like a boy. And, mind you, when a girl tries to catch anything in her lap she throws her knees apart; she don't clap them together, the way you did when you catched the lump of lead. Why, I spotted you for a boy when you was threading the needle; and I contrived the other things just to make certain*. These are the qualities of a real, genu-*wine* girl, a girl born on and who has remained on this side.

It happens when you are approached, like I was, by a man out front of the basketball courts you intended on walking past without even averting your gaze from the ground. Conway, we called the basketball court, where you used to play H-O-R-S-E with your cousin before he got tall as shit and where you played three games of summer league basketball before realizing you hate basketball. When you, like I was, are fifteen years old and a man—"P" was his name, he says—stops you and engages you in conversation you think is simply friendly. Somehow, he finds his way to asking you, "You know what training girls means?" And you don't, but you think you do, so you tell him it's when you get a girl [*sic*] to do what you want without question. He smirks and tells you no, it's when "you and your niggas run a train on a chick, one after another." And you just nod, wanting to leave. He asks if you're a virgin, and you lie, because an affirmative answer is an unacceptable answer. You are fifteen and you should be getting pussy by now, how else do you expect to become a man, which you have no choice but to become, they tell you. This is how you become a proper man, is what he's telling you with his questions, importantly a man who reps this side with ardor. He tries so hard to heterosexualize you because he knows, implicitly, that is how he can make you (and no doubt himself, too) align seamlessly. Your alignment, your cisness, is inextricable from these questions, as he knows, implicitly, *the presumption of sex/gender alignment and its continuity with desire is most centrally connected to the heterosexual imperative*—an imperative he utterly demands of you or else you cannot leave his presence.[5] Your unenthusiasm does not impress him, so he tries to make you a man. "Here, put my number in your phone," he says. "You remember my name, right?" and you almost forgot but remembered the single letter of his name before it became too awkward to respond with anything other than yes. "I'mma have one of my bitches hit you up."

Back then, I didn't believe him, I was just happy he let me leave after that, after giving him dap. I don't remember my destination, but that is no matter, because I went home the long way right after that. And sure enough, I get a text as I sat on the living room couch. One of his "bitches." P was making me an aligned man, getting me the pussy I should have had by now. I didn't respond to the text.

This is all to say that it happens in the small, quotidian moments. It accumulates with each comment, each reprimand, each coercive pull from others and solidifies itself on your being. Sometimes, most times, you don't notice it. But the imperceptible coercive pulling makes you do things you didn't know you were doing, then the things it's making you do feel like simply things you want to do, things it's only natural to do. What is all the fuss? I've been doing this for years, just being me, just being the man that my god made me and every other man who is a man because they are men. We are just being the girls, the women we've always been. It is the most natural thing in the world that I love to do girly things—and girly is as girly does, has always been its girly self, self-same across time and space and universe. What is the need for all this feminism, this talk about gender? We have been this way since we were born. What is the big deal?

There is no big deal, really, mostly. It's a lot of small deals. So many small deals that stitch together what we call big deals, which are, again, many tiny and not-so-tiny small deals. And that is what all this feminism, all this talk about gender, is in part about: refusing the small deals when they happen, those small deals that are brushed off as jokes or insignificant, though, we know now, they are integral patches of the big deals that we can't say anything about without y'all getting huffy since we didn't say anything about the small deals in the first place. We are rejecting the insidiousness you presume to be various iterations of "making a big deal" because all we are doing is ensuring our and others' survival when you are unable to see the violence you have forged into a voice, a movement of your shoulders, a gait, a presumption.

The blowing up of this Narnia—that secretive place that is under threat of being found out, its existence predicated on, at base, a violence and elision of the alternative worlds out there—may not be so incendiary after all. That is, if one wishes to blow something up, one needs explosives. Explosives, though, are far from the old-timey spherical black bomb with a string fuse. Such a simplistic portrayal of explosives. To blow something up requires an archive of tiny tinkerings that get the bomb to explode. Not one and done; many and always on the verge of disintegrating.

WHAT HAPPENS WHEN (my) blackness and (not my) cis masculinity (or femininity), a cisness nearly always assumed and thus uncommented upon, invisibilized, meet one another? In the vast land of Narnia, there is also a pervasive—and regally instantiated—whiteness, which means: the C-4 rigged to send Narnia to kingdom come is, you know it, a deep, sleek black. How could it not be?

Blowing up Narnia would result in something like the dehumaning, the ungendering, the nega-bodying of what it is we call life and its predicates, what we call the world. This conflagratory project must be one, to my mind, that incorporates the fissuring concatenation of blackness and slights big and small to cisgender, for to disregard the import of race viz (and not viz; differently and more radically excessive of "race") blackness rebukes the radical project sought. Narnia is not only solipsistically cis; it is solipsistically white, which is not merely to call out the White Witch but to take seriously how her sovereign reign pervades the land—how it is not about individuated boogeypeople but, following the legendary Mike Jackson, how we must blame it on the boogie itself.[6]

So what does this urge us to think about Narnia-cum-cisness and whiteness? Think of the blackness I espouse here not as a slathering of the White Witch with melanin; think of it as a kind of ethical, sociopolitical invitation. One in which whiteness as a *fictive line of purity* is undermined by and refused in service of a radical undertaking of unsovereignty, a blackness understood *precisely as opening up an alternate imaginary of the sacred from which also opens up other worlds.*[7] Other worlds, yes; trans worlds, *transworlds* articulable through blackness.[8] Rejecting the world cisgender has erected and made our required birthright means we must reject, therefore, the familial line. Our inheritance is a hefty one, with which comes the reaping of vast sums of wealth acquired on the derogation and decimation of other kinds of bodies and terrains and ways of knowing. We cannot take that inheritance and perpetuate the disparities, the violences, of such wealth accumulation. Cisgender orients us toward what is "right" in the world, an orientation we are called, in our leveling of Narnia, to encounter askance. It matters little, if at all, if we have been given the crown, the scepter, the throne. Those endowments are not definitive, do not lodge us in place, giving us an out. We take the crown off, throw down the scepter, get up from the throne and shout to the good people, *This reign, henceforth, shall be over.*

This familial line is no flippant metaphor. It bears the weight of a history laden with a perverse reappropriation of a serial practice of terror. If we are urged to dissent from familial inheritances, to turn down the familial line, how might this necessitate a reckoning with those blackened chattels who were prohibited familiality itself? Enslaved black subjects did not inherit family lines even though, for all intents and purposes, they were "owed" that. They passed on no wealth, could not be said to possess their offspring. One's children could be sold on a whim, never to be seen again. One's marriage held no legally recognized weight. No ties were sanctioned. *Family*, as a term given through the juridical, was rendered evacuated of meaning in the context of blackness. We can learn from a potent site of blackness the very toxicity of obsession with familial inheritances. Since blackness ruptured normative family ties, ties that, in this analytic account, are attached to a passing down of a reproductive conception of sex and gender tied to their alignment and regulation, there is salvation in reformulating *family* around *kinship*. It is kinship that offers a different conceptual model for how we relate to one another outside the trappings of *family* and its coercive inheritances and expectations to take over the family business. The business is a machine that seeks to reproduce the world as it has long been, to preserve the normative family. To preserve the valor of whiteness; to preserve the staying in line, the regulation of whose genitals meet whose. Blackness invites the swarmy miasma of kinship whose irreverence to the juridical ties of the family allow for wayward maneuvers unable to be mapped, unable to align neatly, unable to remain on this side.

What might this say about possibilities for different kinds of life? It is no secret that C. S. Lewis was a Christian dedicated to the purpose of making his faith both seen and heard. And I have been an atheist for a while now. The first book of his seven-book Chronicles is threaded with Christian moralism, symbolic iterations of biblical stories, and sets up a Narnian version of the crucifixion and resurrection through Aslan's messianic offer to give his life to save others. That is the narrative, a distinctly Christo-theological one, and if it buttresses cisnormativity in my extension of the metaphoric equation, then to blow up Narnia is to usher in a Luciferian nocturne.

DAD USED TO SAY that I was a prince because I was his only child, destined to inherit his money, his possessions, even his wardrobe (which he constantly tried to pawn off on me, despite my staunch departure from his old-man-trying-to-be-hip-and-cool style). I never took to the language for some unknown reason; it always landed askew, its gendered regality sitting quite uncomfortably with me. I am not surprised in hindsight that I have not spoken with my father in seven years.

But the language appeared to me again some fifteen years later in Jared Sexton's *Black Men, Black Feminism: Lucifer's Nocturne*.[9] Where the *imago dei* is to bring light, Lucifer is to bring a nocturnal salvation of sorts. The figure for such a salvation, though, incarnated away from supernatural conjurings, is the "Dark Prince." Drawing on Michael Hardt and Antonio Negri's notion of the new Prince, who emerges on the horizon not as an individual messiah, much less a political party or figurehead of leadership, but as *the political articulation that weaves together the different forms of resistance and struggles for liberation in society today. This Prince thus appears as a swarm, a multitude moving in coherent formation and carrying, implicitly, a threat.*[10] But if this Prince augurs a demonic and democratic threat, it is necessarily, for Sexton, "a Dark Prince" (19), he(?) who profanes the throne and divine Glory. If the king owns and verifies everything the light touches, if it is all Mufasa's domain bequeathed unto Simba bequeathed unto Simba's son and so on, alteration of which would amount to divine treason of the hierarchically taxonomic decree, then there is only possibility for salvation in the nontaxonomic through the darkness. The image of god has dictated what is to be considered life, terrestrially and extraterrestrially—that is, the afterlife. What, then, is life that profanes this life?

Which is another way of saying, or rather asking, what is life—what are *we*—when we are no longer in, on *this side* of, Narnia? There is a particular way that in the problematizing of the "cis" in cisgender, *and* the "gender" in cisgender, blackness promulgates demonic thinking. Narnia's predication on the theologics Lewis could not live without have orchestrated viable life in a certain way. A Luciferian nocturne, a darkened prince that is not a prince because my youthful discomfort with its designation implies the insufficiency, the violence, of both its gender and its monarchicality, brings about another way to do life outside of the gender that has touted itself as gender in toto. The disjuncture between blackness and cisgender is instructive of other modes of life that foreground *forms of life independent of the trappings of sovereign power, including the hallmarks of conventional manhood and the structures of kinship linked to its presumptive centrality—paterfamilias* (19). Over here, we eat angels—wings and all—in between meals. I did not want the manhood implied by the "prince," indexical of the pillars upholding Narnia; indeed, I did not want it because it could not claim me as I was too smitten with a blackness that rejected the violence of the binary on which the "manhood" was predicated. I did not want *family*, indexical of the paternal line, that ceremonial instantiation so beholden to regulating reproduction and accumulating wealth in the form of the feminine, the monetary, the status—the paterfamilias. My own discomfort attuned me to the salvific discomfort that trans's shade-throwing on cis made known in other realms. That discomfort and that shade, the folks who did that work, they were kinfolk, and I wanted to—still want to—be with them, cuttin' *up* in atheologics and nocturnologies. All I really wanted, really want, is for us to see how Narnia's demise is gotten at by, no doubt among other kinfolk they tried to keep us from, the *problematiz[ing]* of *the very notion of men and women as a class* (50) that blackness engenders and the *troubl[ing]* of *the categories of binary gender and of medically assigned sex for their historical and contemporary violences* that (trans)gender, that the trans, engenders.[11]

: : :

Blowing up Narnia is, and can only be, the task of the black and noncis, the black and (trans)gender, and that is to say, too, that those who take on that task move with the groove of the black and noncis, the black and (trans)gender, inasmuch as these are projects, not coveted and exclusionary identities. I am cutting all of us some slack, but only in exchange for making the rope immensely difficult to hold. You are no longer, by way of cisgender's (bio)logical shit show, condemned to your assignation, your body, for these do not determine you. But in this undetermination, you are tasked—rigorously, quotidianly tasked—with a critical examination and constant work. Those of us who have been thrown outside, however minimally, by the normative binary (the blacks, the butch lesbians, the sissy men, the enbies, the queers, the freaks) *may not be all that "cis," as conventionally understood by trans and queer scholars and activists*, or by those who giddily band together under its heading. And this is because we do not want to simply uphold and venerate difference; we want to destroy that which creates the powers that instruct how we are to hierarchize difference. So the refusal of doubling down on our purported cis genders as a way to buy into power, to get cozy with The Man, which nevertheless tames the edgy edges of gender by *merely positing and protecting difference*, is in service not of absolving privileges; it is in service, first and foremost, always, of *critiquing the constitutive nature of power*.[12] Which is to say, becoming kinfolk with the black and (trans)gender.

# RE: [NO SUBJECT]

X <x@undisclosedlocation.[dis]org> Thu, Feb. 20, 2020
11:22 AM

To me

to whom it may concern:

deep breath. its been a minute since i returned to this question in a sustained way. standing in the way was much frustration & insecurity, feeling that i was not permitted to think & say what im going to think & say, then getting mad that there was something out there making me feel like i couldnt think & say the things i wanted to think & say. but here i am, thinking & saying. with a bit of a vengeance.

what i am thinking & saying concerns gender. but thats no surprise, especially to you. but perhaps more specifically genders discontents that go under the heading of trans & nonbinary. if i may. though oftentimes i know i may not. per my last message, which may have gotten lost in your inbox, there has been an increase in the questions weight, not because of some seismic shift in the social landscape but because, i gather, you have been forced to grapple. though thats not really true. youve long grappled, its just that your grappling has come to a head, as they say; your grappling can no longer be grappled with alone. if it ever could.

youve grappled so much youve begun to tear at the seams you thought—because so many people made it appear this way—were not seams at all but just the objective curvature of your body. but youve been thinking & reading, listening & writing, learning & giving yourself over to the enticingly liberatory call of otherwise genders, otherwise ways of life & living. theyve beckoned you, these ways, & youve uncloaked all those covered-over seams & sutures within yourself. & now your opening is getting you into beautiful, thorny, mellifluous trouble.

so you are trying to escape your body. trying, not because you dislike it; you are trying to escape the thing, your body, that everyone else continues to tell you is simply there. it is lashed with so much, so much unfamiliarity. & they believe that it was there all along, before they showed up. like theyre just telling you, in speedometer-like fashion, how fast you were going when they are the ones who forced your foot onto the pedal & made up the concepts of miles & hours. i am writing to sit with you & listen to how you will exit from an enveloping corporeal masculinity while knowing full well—both of us do—that it is unclear how far youll get away with it. because we know *winking face*, & i think they know too & simply do not admit it, that bodies signify nothing; *physiology is nothing without meaning*, & those *meanings do not cling to bodies like some kind of glutinous vapor or semiotic paste.*[1] there are subtle crimes that occur when they bring hes to you, when they require your participation, on ethical grounds no less, in he-ing yourself—a he-ing that expands so much farther than an anatomical assessment. when they do this, they are committing semiotic crimes, crimes of meaning-making that snatch your body from you, forcing you to recognize yourself perpetually in the ways only theyve sanctioned.

what you want is unspecific nonrecognition.

until soon,

X

X <x@undisclosedlocation.[dis]org> Sat, Feb. 22, 2020
4:03 PM

To me

to whom it may concern:

i really didnt feel like writing you today, again . . .

there are many, many reserves & questions folks have of nonbinary (non)gender (non)identity. (not least because of weird lexical constructions like *[non]gender* & *[non]identity.*) like that nonbinariness skews "masculine" since femme gender expressions, because of, you know, misogyny, are cast as "extra" things one adds to a supposedly natural state; theres a simmering assumption that nonbinariness is to dress & express in ways that would be read as a muted masculinity, for its the assumption that femininity is definitionally contrived or frivolous which then implies the naturalness & sincerity of masculinity. so, theres that *shrug*. theres also the presumption that nonbinariness is a privilege only afforded to those proximal to whiteness, since nonbinariness is seen as itself a privilege possessed only by those not subject to needing gender as a vector through which to gain personhood, the case for many people of color. & then still, theres just plain ol cisnormativity, & the belief that to refuse gender is yet another way to absolve oneself of privilege. its hard sometimes to get out of those assumptions. that is the treacherous archive one brings with them when daring to emerge through the nonbinary, needing to sift through all those layers of far-from-perfect-&-in-fact-quite-harmful meaning. nonbinariness is a fight in many ways, because to want to rid oneself of the violence inherent in the imposition of gender (is that simply to say gender? hmm . . .) is to make oneself vulnerable to the immediate, ruthless imposition of gender.

its like you never really mean it when you respond to the question of your gender—if others are kind enough to even pose it as a question, which is rare—with "nonbinary." youre not lying, of course. its only that thats the closest approximation right now to what it is you dont simply feel. theres a bit of a stranglehold that feeling has on validating ones gender identity—ive *felt* this way ever since i can remember; if thats how you *feel*, then its valid. which is cool, i guess. i dont really have beef with that. but what of the validity of ones subjectivity as it may relate to gender when that subjectivity might also be based on ones thought, ones politicality, ones desire for something not-yet? can we be nonbinary even if we dont all the way feel it but damn sure think it, yearn for it, want it proliferated throughout the world as a dormant detonator to the gender binary?

because what you really want to say when they ask the question "how do you identify?" which they do when being polite or genuinely opening space for you, because that happens too, is: *i dont.*

& i promise i heard you loud & clear when you expressed to me in not ~~so~~ many words that none of this is selfish. its really, really not. it is not to be absolved of privilege nor is it to make things simpler for yourself nor is it to fit in now that being nonbinary is "cool." no, no, no, thats not it at all. part of it is because, as Audre Lorde has written in an unpublished poem, which is to say a poem that could not be ensnared by the affixing filigree of publications that might have done editorial violence to it, *we seek beyond history for a new and more possible meeting.* they keep trying to bring history to our subjective doors, & that makes sense. but what were trying to do is become something more than history, for history is the site of so many violences that we are forced to live; we are seeking a way to live that does not reject history per se but knows that we are & can be, & must be, more than historys weight.

everyone knows . . . —actually, thats such a lie. anytime someone says something like that. its a lie. theres no way to truthfully complete the sentence "everybody knows . . ." so, my bad. *many of us know* that there arent, or shouldnt be, any specific rules for seeking to do ones identity in excess of the gender binary. there is no metric for the percentage of which you must signify masculine & feminine, & there is no nonbinary uniform. we know this. but we dont often believe this & dont often hold ourselves & others to manifesting this. i wonder if the urge to make us all check proverbial boxes & measure up to a nebulous standard the criteria of which even the makers of the standard dont fully grasp is a testament to how disingenuous we are sometimes. & im not even thinking about the easy punching bags: right-wingers, conservatives, well-meaning liberals, nice white ladies, hypothetical strawpeople. no, i mean even the folks in our radical movement spaces. we say we want to burn it all down, that we want to end the world as we know it & abolish white supremacy & prisons & heteropatriarchy. but do we truly mean that? is that something we are ready for? because that would entail, as Fred Moten says, the *absolute overturning, the absolute turning of this motherfucker out*; it would entail racial & gender abolition—thoroughgoing abolition—& the impossibility of knowing ahead of time the identification of the being before us & the tortuously elegant openness to having our assumptions undermined & the utter cessation of biological, binaristic, sociohistorical determinism. like, how can they insist that i, you, we, double down on the immutable fact of our gender, that we cannot be, say, nonbinary if we look exactly like a cis dude (next time ask them the criteria by which this is arrived at), when we are trying to abolish prisons, which buttress & proliferate the logics of the gender binary; when we are trying to eradicate colonialism, of which gender serves as an embedded object & concrete colonial practice; when we are trying to be accomplices & not just allies, which belies the co-conspiratorial call to not only support the crime but commit the crime, to not only celebrate the struggle but be in & get sullied by the struggle; when we say "Down with capitalism!" which is inextricable from hypermasculinist patriarchal privatizing of femme bodies & capacities & is antithetical to a project of radical gender abolition the aim of which nonbinariness as a political strategy & subjective deployment is in service? riddle me all of that, jack.

sorry if my tone is snarky or dismissive. i dont mean to be. its just that you are one of those beings who yearn not to flit from one category to a different category but to in fact wholly escape, & that is hard on others. & who can blame them? this isnt something theyve prepared for nor is it something readily recognizable as liberatory. & maybe thats the point.

in coalition & solidarity,

X

X <x@undisclosedlocation.[dis]org> Thu, Feb. 24, 2020
11:22 AM

To me

to whom it may concern:

it was my—our—junior year of high school, remember? you were thoroughly fed up with football & its dudeness, high school students who had the rudest of attitudes. you had just gotten a facebook too, not of your own accord, but decided to keep it because, why not? after school one day you were mad bored, scrolling timelines, then DMed about five people. some were friends, others acquaintances. only one responded, the cute 4′10″ girl you met at mikes house a few weeks prior while yall were playing volleyball in his backyard. M. she was kind, asked how football was going. she knew you played because her brother played too his senior year, your sophomore year, the year before he died, at college, a botched routine mechanical tutorial. you said you were tired of football, didnt feel like going to practice every day, didnt care about the fanfare of the games. & besides, the season was just about wrapping up, yall being nowhere close to playoffs. & then she asked the question that catapulted the response you thought nothing of, the response that made her continue talking.

*so, now that football is over, you going bitty hunting?* a "bitty," for those of you unfamiliar with that 2008 lingo, is the name given to a girl or woman evacuated of personhood outside of romantic or sexual fulfillment. a bitty is, in short, a girl or woman unto sex with you. *i dont want a bitty*, you responded, *i want a girlfriend.*

you started dating a few weeks after that moment. ill spare the details of high school romance & awkwardness, because thats not the point of the story. the point of the story is that six & a half months elapsed before you & her, as the 2008 (well, it was 09 at this point) lingo went, "got with each other." at month four, though, there had been rumblings. she told your mutual friends that no funny business had occurred yet &, as she told it to you after, they laughed. how could yall not have done anything yet, they wondered. whats wrong with "him." you, looking as you did—just a slightly smaller version of how you look now, with less hair on your head than now, about a dozen fewer tattoos, but generally the same musculature, the same face, the same disposition of timidity & anxiety & insecurity—were expected to be jumping at the chance to be sexual, to do the manly thing of sexually conquering her. you were not performing to the level you were supposed to. because you were a man & as a man, or someone growing into a man & expected to claim, unequivocally, manhood, you must unsheathe that manhood by vociferously desiring sex, now, without fear, without question. spill your manhood over her & shout its spillage to others.

but you did not want to, not yet. you did not want to be coerced or expected; you did not feel a rush. & perhaps, in hindsight, it was your lack of desire to be the man they demanded of you. but that has consequences, we know. a guy you had known for a few years, a guy who called you his brother, which meant something to you, had Ms number. they were friends, you thought. but M forwarded you the texts he sent her after he, too, discovered your failure to be, to do, the man you were supposed to. *what you need is a real nigga who can give you what you need. if he aint giving it to you, then best believe i can. and we aint even gotta tell him. just sayin.*

years later you read a poem, "Sexual History," in which Billy-Ray Belcourt, beautifully queer & indigenous, writes about a girl he dated in eighth grade. you dated a girl in eleventh grade. the parents of the girl Belcourt dated in eighth grade said that he was "not manly enough for her." the friends of the girl you dated in eleventh grade did not think you were manly enough, did not think you adequately performed your manliness; the friend of yours who you thought was also a friend of hers, who called you his brother, did not think you were manly enough & that he could be, that he was, more manly than you. & he could prove it. Belcourt felt differently then, & certainly feels differently now, about the accusations of lacking manliness. he is "relieved," he says, gracefully, "to be neither wildfire nor prison cell." if only you felt differently then, though you certainly feel differently now, about the accusations & demonstrations of your lacking manliness. you wanted not to spread that wildfire you were long tasked with stoking, called a bad arsonist if those flames were extinguished. but you do not wish to cause further destruction. how could you have told them that you did not jump when they said jump because you were, blessedly, floating in the middle of somewhere else, some other kind of terrain without the solidity of the terra grounding their assertions? you did not want to slay & conquer & dominate. you did not want to be coerced or expected to carry a banner the nation of which you wanted to rebuke but didnt know how, or that you could. you wanted to escape the prison cell they told you was home. & they didnt let you. why?

you can think of many answers now, & a handful back then. it still makes you sad. but one bright spot is that ever since then, long before & after then, you never stopped, in small ways, tunneling out with a spoon.

keep tunneling,

X

X <x@undisclosedlocation.[dis]org> Wed Feb. 26, 2020 9:11 AM

To me

to whom it may concern:

i went to bed last night thinking about something you shared with me the other day. something about gender & social constructs & all that. this isnt new at all, though usually my gender thinking is reserved for the daylight hours. it kept me up. or, it kept me between, vacillating in a swarming slush of musing. people often just say "gender is a social construct" like they just left their intro to gender studies class as undergrad sophomores. & then there are the undergrad juniors who retort, "yeah, but that doesnt mean it doesnt have material effects" like theyre so much more enlightened. *yawn.*

its such a boring conversation to me, to us, i think. i need more than those oft-mentioned quips because it does nothing to subvert powers grasp on our very lives. it doesnt account for *how* & *by whom* & *for what purposes* gender has been constructed; &, the retort often doesnt consider the nontransparency of materiality (or, that "material effects" does not have obvious meaning nor is such materiality extricated from the discursivity—the constructedness—of gender nor, one more gain, do those "effects" signify [cis] "woman" always & without internal variation).

i am less interested, which is not to say noninterested, in simply reiterating the injustices done toward noncis men, as if enumeration is the end-all be-all of justice. i am interested in fucking this whole shit up because this whole shit is fucked up.

so what does that look like? in a word, it is radical trans politics, it is radical black trans feminist politics toward racialized gender abolition. (well, thats more than "a" word.) all of this entails so much more than wearing "the future is female" shirts, wanting women ceos & presidents & representation representation REPRESENTATION, or "celebrating" womens "empowerment." we are not about fighting for discrete, individual rights or insertion into a representational logic that is never neutral & always coded along racial & gender lines; we are about fighting the very machinery that doles out rights & is coeval with violence. the politicality to which we must ascribe is to fight this cultural machinery which categorizes, stigmatizes, & then marginalizes minorities, so it is not a matter of simply being pro-woman, pro-black, pro-lgbt. much of what has come to pass as feminist discourse & activism, as well as black liberation & freedom struggle, has been in fact to foreclose liberatory avenues. we have come to *fixing and stabilizing the identity of woman [&, too, black, trans, queer] even more firmly than before*. what if, & im just spitballing here, the engine of our politics followed Riki Wilchins, that treacherously menacing transsexual radical, if they forged an unruly beast of a movement with the *unapologetically black and unapologetically transgender* Marshall Green? this is to say, i want a subjective politicality that emerges at the nexus of Wilchins, who writes,

> Some women become indistinguishable from men. Some women become more distinguishable from women. Some fall off that specious male-female spectrum entirely, becoming totally new genders we haven't yet named. Possibilities which our original feminism could not have foreseen or anticipated are created. Fluidity is transformed into a key feminist goal and an important liberatory tactic.

> Our movement shifts its foundations from identity to one of functions of oppression. Coalitions form around particular issues, and then dissolve. Identity becomes the result of contesting those oppressions, rather than a precondition for involvement. In other words, identity becomes an effect of political activism instead of a cause.[2]

& Green, who writes, asking incisive & necessary questions,

> What do your politics look like? And what kind of work do you do? . . .
>
> The gender binary is troubled and it is challenged. It is not only or always transgender people that we recognize as simply (or not so simply) moving from one place on the gender binary to another that do the troubling. There are many people for which transition isn't just a moment and time to be completed. Some people live and reside outside or fluctuate between genders—this critique is one that collapses binaries. . . .
>
> I would and I do choose to be black as long as black holds this possibility of fugitivity and the desire to escape hegemonic control and order.[3]

how we move toward our politics comes to serve as identities, identities that are not preconditions but forged in the process of imaging our work & our politics. that is what it must mean when we foreground the black & feminist & queer & trans—foregrounding certain kinds of work. this work dissolves the footholds we commonly believe we need in order to do the work. to say yes to that desire to escape hegemonic control & order. even at the level of the body.

so its a different kind of "wrong body" narrative. beautiful hordes of trans folks have dismantled the efficacy of the wrong body narrative, arguing over & over again that it just doesnt cut it. what im talking about is the way nonbinary gender commitments assert the wrong-ish-ness of the very move to classify bodies along lines of (binary) gender. it is an assertion that *bodies* are wrong. before the materialists come after me, i know, kinda, that we "have" bodies. flesh & bone there is, of course, so save yourself the unsheathing of that phrase against me like ive never heard it before. ive heard it; it is nothing new. so dont even start.

these people gravely overlook that the "body," too, & the things that stem from it, are not given to us unmediated. we must recognize that *our epistemological certainty about our own bodies is not given, but is delivered by processes and interactions . . . that connect us to the world through which we move*, Gayle Salamon argues. encountering the world & our very phenomenological, existential inhabitation of ourselves is always mediated, & that mediation shapes not only *our knowledge of our bodies but our feelings in them as well.*[4]

nonbinariness & the trans feminist politics it carries with it is an assault on how we come to know who any"body" is. it is not necessarily a "visual" confirmation so much as a stalwart subjective flexion that implies that we are corralled into confining grammars of surveillance, policing, & circumscription impeding full-scale liberation. i come to nonbinariness from more than a certain kind of feeling. it has been arrived at by me, via refusing to say "that *guy* over there," via balking at the assumption that a body necessarily implies a specific gender, via not being on my way to another choice given to us & instead wanting neither the gender they gave me nor the "other" gender—*I'm not on my way anywhere*, Harry Dodge told Maggie Nelson, *I do not want the female gender . . . Neither do I want the male gender . . . I don't want any of it.*[5]

so often our beloved enbies get maligned because we apparently do not recognize that the house we occupy, this embodied framing, has a certain architecture. it takes up space in a certain way, strikes the eye in certain ways, is on land that would be open if it werent for the shape of that architecture. we know this, & *from*, not *to the exclusion of*, this knowing we steadfastly assert ourselves *anarchitecturally*, as my buddy Jack Halberstam would say. thanks, Jack.

& thanks to you,

X

X <x@undisclosedlocation.[dis]org> Wed Feb. 26, 2020
9:39 PM

To me

to whom it may concern:

*pronoun*: late middle english: from *pro-* "on behalf of" + *noun*, suggested by french *pronom*, latin *pronomen* (from *pro-* "for, in place of" + *nomen* "name"). a word that can function as a noun phrase used by itself & that refers either to the participants in the discourse (e.g., i, you) or to someone or something mentioned elsewhere in the discourse (e.g., she, it, this).

whats in a pronoun? its growing more commonplace to hear the question "what pronouns do you use?" & i love it. though some dont, thinking it to be liberal millennial hogwash or coerced "outing." but i like it not so much for its ritualistic nature—it does feel sometimes that its asked as a way to appear down for the trans cause (as if only trans people have pronouns)—but for its opening. to ask the question presents the possibility of responding with something unexpected, or, too, with nothing at all. & in the wake of that, how do we respond? do we force a choice in the form of he, she, or if theyre generous they; or do we take whatever is offered, letting it slowly cultivate the texture of another kind of world?

pronouns, those units of language so potent with signification, so meaningful in the contemporary lexicon (& for good reason). pronouns are like tiny vessels of verification that others are picking up what youre putting down. &, theyre timid requests of others to say yes, i see you, & even if you are imaged in the likeness of something ive yet to see, i see that ive not yet seen you, but i still, now, will love you.

i think you are taking that & running with it. because you & your pronouns are embattled. not in a bellicose lexical standoff, but by virtue of the tension that they must convey. but others often want something definitive, & if not definitive, familiar. you must *look* nonbinary or else you are just trying to relinquish yourself of your cis privilege. you must be identifiable *as trans* in order to claim that you are trans, or that you face transantagonism. these imperfect terms we have diligently forged come with terms & conditions, & that is understandable, really it is. so you begin to feel compelled to fall in line, to be what they see, which is often not you, but is what others see so that is what you have to capitulate to because youre read in a certain way & encountered in a certain way & thats how you must be, they say, imply, want you to believe. you begin to believe that others are the arbiters of who you think you are &, more importantly, who you are permitted to be.

maybe this is all to say that sometimes, perhaps even oftentimes, the doubt & invalidation is coming from *inside* the house.

maybe the issue lies on the horizon to which youre looking. you see what dips across the pinnacle into a landless land, where nongenders & ultragenders roam, while youre still (said to be) standing in the land of reality, they call it. do not dare think unreal thoughts or structure your adamant assertion of yourself on unrealistic grounds. you are to stay here, right here, in reality, where things have been this way for a while & we dont care if you wish they were otherwise because, oh, well, honey, you have to just deal with the facts, with matter, with the fact of the matter. & others are in this land too (theyre the ones telling you all these things), knowing fully that this land is where they are & must keep their eyes on, no time for dreaming because dreamers get killed & dreamers dont see clearly & dreamers think that all is fine because theyre too busy thinking about what might be even though *might* is just another word for *isnt yet*.

you, my friend, are a dreamer nonetheless.

but why dream? maybe because that is what you are presenting them with when they ask your pronouns. you are gifting them with an unreality that might shake them from the terrors of waking life. you wish to, in your nonbinariness or your indifference or your refusal, hold imposed ascriptions in abeyance—in a move toward radical self-*un*determination—so you can facilitate a different kind of encounter. or, the abeyance, the gendered indeterminacy, interrogates the very grounds on which (gendered) relations occur, shifting the terrain toward alternative modes of relationality not predicated on *sirs* & *maams* & *bros* & *ladies* & *gentlemen*. & that requires nothing but a wish & a desire for something else.

where you are, my beloved friend, is *in the basement mixin up the medicine with the wizard of id* because *it delivers us from the grip of the grid*. you listened to this line in an Aesop Rock song—"Save Our Ship"—& were sent adrift on some experimental lines, or tremors, of thought as you drove home along lakeshore drive. in an underground dwelling (the basement), dark & subterranean, you tinker & experiment (mixin up) like the inheritor of that Ellisonian "thinker-tinker" that you are, mix & match & unmatch things up, with a magical wizard in the likeness of id (that Freudian subjective area not beholden to the chronos or decorum or taxonomy of society). i have no doubt that it is dark down there in the basement, no doubt that it is hard to see, though you do not need to see, might be impeded in your experimentation were you to be seeing things. the darkness facilitates feeling, a different way to feel & be in collaboration with others, a different way that means you are now, finally, able to mix it up. what are yall mixing up? what funky brews are yall concocting? actually, dont tell me. i like surprises. all i know, which is why im so happy & excited—chuffed, as the brits would say—is that whatever is yielded will deliver us from the vice-like grip of the grid: the cordoned, the discrete, the categorical, the legible, the known & possible. keep on mixing it up.

i think i might have found something that captures what all this might mean. something that captures this gender so elusive & not-itself. something that captures the radical obliteration you want to emerge into. thats the gender you want. & i found the perfect thing to express that. please see attached.

best,

X

X <x@undisclosedlocation.[dis]org> Wed Feb. 26, 2020 9:42 PM

To me

the file was too large . . .

with apologies, & thanks,

X

X <x@undisclosedlocation.[dis]org> Sat Mar. 7, 2020 9:39 AM

To me

to whom it may concern:

can emails have epigraphs?

**I don't know if he was one. And if he was, in fact, a cis man, I have no idea how long he'll remain one. Gender is never fixed; gender is always broken.—Sophia Giovannitti, "In Defense of Men," 2020**

ive been thinking about this a lot with some of our friends. i texted D the other day. i asked if D had ever read those Foucault lectures compiled into a book titled *Wrong-Doing, Truth-Telling* &, after sending a screenshot of the books summary—detailing the role of avowal & confession as they relate to subject constitution—D responded & our co-constitutive subjective weaving commenced:

Sent from my mobile. [A mobility constitutive of the subject who sent it as well]

X: Have you read this book? I feel a strong compulsion to buy it immediately lol

D: I have not seen it (or read it)! But it looks quite interesting
Hmmm I might really need to get it.

X: You should, & I will too, then we should talk about it. I think I told you that lately I've been thinking about myself, blackness, (nonbinary) gender, the category of cisgender, & I find myself super interested in the nonconsensual "confession" coaxed from certain gendered bodies & the possibility of foreclosing the purported confession, or how one might refuse to confess (cis)gender especially when the confession is demanded

D: I have /*feelings*/ about nonconsensual confessions of gender position

X: I'd love to know those feelings! ☺

D: I have just always felt resistant to the compulsory demand to express my gender nonbinariness by social justice advocates (whom I usually don't have a problem with). But if I don't confess, they chalk me up to a cis white man. & I am not . . . cis, & I'm biracial, though I am aware I pass as white. It's just all very frustrating

In general I've been feeling a lot of grief toward the self-righteousness certain social justice movements are imbued with, lately. I think it's dangerous. I'm sympathetic with the goals, obviously, but the methods are starting to worry me

Does any of that make sense?

X: It does! We should have a longer conversation about this at some point. But I am VERY MUCH in line with where you're at. & social justice orgs are sometimes, to me, trash. The /*feelings*/ are mutual

To be committed to nonbinariness (as both of us are; I've been flitting between pronouns & sociopolitical genders for a while) is, to me, very much a refusal of many of the subtle logics of violence supposed radicals in fact clutch so dearly. Which is frustrating

D: Oof. Wow, we really are in sync. We definitely need to have a talk sometime about this. I've been feeling very stuck precisely because of this issue

Well said

X: Like seriously. I've been thinking about this stuff a lot. & idk how to navigate it off the page. The page is easy, people are hard

D: Preaching to the choir. I've been having a rough go with some people in my department precisely due to this

& thank you for always seeking to understand me, friend—your simple acceptance & interest in my "non-"ness is refreshing & strengthening. You do not try to place me in preconceived categories

X: Of course! We come from & have traveled along such complementary intellectual & political traditions, so it feels that it was nearly inevitable. Plus, the categorical—those "given ontologies"—is a profound violence. And I refuse to proliferate violence, especially toward you

D: You da best ☺

maybe we were too hard & sweeping, too homogenizing & monolithic, with respect to activist circles. theyre not all bad, of course. & they do great work. &, too, im not always the most pleasant person to deal with. so, not all orgs & all that.

yet i do kind of stand by what we expressed. sometimes the very conditions of participation are such that interrogation of those conditions portends a threat to the whole edifice. & that provokes fear, rightly so. why would you want to invite in someone who will bring about your destruction? i get that. but the destruction is necessary, constant ungrounding is necessary, for that is radical trans/feminist politics, to my mind; to remain, as ones very feminist practice, vigilant as to the ground on which we stand. it is the call we must heed constantly, for feminist radicality, trans politicality, queer politics, nonbinary thinking, whatever term you wish to deploy, is actualized at the precise moment when it is vanquished by the very people (or nonpeople, not-quite-people) who are excluded from the term & yet who justifiably expect to be part of it, by those whose political vocabulary may carry different lexical commitments yet similar political commitments. all i was trying to say is that their politics cannot be fixed & settled once & for all, & that their very politics—their professed politics of radicality & abolition—are in fact the product of a perpetual interrogation of the grounds of politics.

i think D understood this. D felt this too. notice Ds ellipsis after "& I am not . . . cis" right before D, hesitatingly, writes "cis." that ellipsis is potent with significatory meaning; that grammatical operation is where D is, in the gendered (& racialized) abeyance, the refusal to announce, to confess oneself nonconsensually *or* consensually, to avow the purported, static "truth" of ones gender. that is what we are both railing against, that compulsory confession we are coaxed into providing when we do not wish to, do not think we can, do not think we should confess that which is untrue & contrary to the open playground of a world we are trying to live here, now, always.

to emerge through nonbinariness is to feel "stuck," as D says. stuck in that we are constantly being brought back to the violent place we hoped to leave. & the bringing back is shrouded in an uncritical good, as if bringing us back is part of their duty as righteous people in the world. do not stray, for that will abnegate the privilege you have—indeed, that we demand that you not only have but that you recite, over & over, that you have. nonbinariness is not a renunciation of the privileges ascribed to the contortions of our bodies. we know very well how we are read somatically, boy do we know. & we know that means something. we are, precisely, trying to interrogate that meaning, trying to challenge the automatic affixation of what we mean on the grounds that we do not wish to mean what you say we mean, & we do not want you, anyone, to mean what others say you mean. to have someone or something say what you mean before "you" even arrive onto the scene—which is to say, to have someone or something dictate the very possibility & boundaries of "you"—is a profound violence of ontological proportions. & we are trying to mitigate violence.

our commitment, Ds & mine—& yours too, my friend—is one that takes brutally seriously the radical theorizing of nonbinary refusals of gender as a violent regime. &, that theorizing loves the world we yearn for so much that those who take on the task start to look like beings that would live in that world. but heres the thing: it is difficult to live in two worlds, or to begin living in another world while still being subject to the terrestrial mandates of this world. some might say youre being unrealistic, which you are. because you have come to know a different real.

i cant help but plan conspiracies with D. because thats what were doing, what weve been doing: trying to peek through into ourselves as refusals of the binary unfloors so many people. it is not whimsical, as some might castigate nonbinary genders—a passing fad all the rage with teeny-boppers & millennials, they say; youll grow out of it, they say—but is meticulously planned, studied, thought, felt. we are not so fixated on constantly positioning, as it seems others are. we dont really want to *be* anywhere, & simply because we are placed, fixed, *be*ed by others does not hold sway over how we should move. we know its important; its just not the world we want. & we are doing nothing but trying vociferously to live the world we seek.

& yet they still balk. because of this it feels so deeply that we are seen as problems to politics, we dont do politics right; we do not follow the policy put forth, becoming distractions, defectors, threats to the cause. this is of ontological proportions; this is about our lives &, not only our living lives, our material livelihood, but about the very conditions on which life happens. what happens when we commit to refusing the proliferation of cisness, refusing its hold over us irrespective of how our bodies register, which is to say, committing to gender abolition & an axiomatic deviation from the belief that ones gender can be evaluatively procured by way of visual assessment, which scarily mimics cisnormative logics?

it is no wonder that when we say we are not what they think we are, in the face of their demand to make us, to require us to be, cis, to them it must have genuinely felt like losing the ground below their feet. that is the life of nonbinariness.

wishing you life,

X

X <x@undisclosedlocation.[dis]org> Sat Mar. 7, 2020 9:39 AM

To me

to whom it may concern:

sigh.

what this is all really about, if it can be "really" "about" anything—as that phrase is so hubristic, implying a fundamentality that the groundlessness & abolitionist spirit of nonbinariness rejects—is a desire to deviate away from, to undermine, the ways that masculinity has been conscripted onto the body you are said to have. & thats whats so difficult to others, & yourself, sometimes: they *see* you being a man, you cant get away from it. they *know* you get goodies & proverbial (& literal) backpats for the extent to which various iterations of "male" privilege (a slippery misnomer, as it cannot be assumed that male = masculine or man, & few of the privileges received are because of ones chromosomes, ones genital configuration, or ones internal plumbing) slather onto you. so you try to get away from it, shun it, because you dont see any good in it. & you reject its assumed conflation with your body, though you know that is where others locate it. but you dont, you cant, & its not your fault your body looks like it does. cant you behead masculinity without beheading yourself? cant you & shouldnt you be able to have the body youve grown to be cool with—like, yall are tight, yall have been through some things—without being confined to masculinity? what of the possibility of knowing intimately what the house of your body means to others & wanting, badly, to murder its curb appeal without changing much of anything but the atmospheric breath surrounding the abode? because masculinity is not simply in your body. nothing, really, is inherent to your body, its all an external affixation, an imposition, & a nonconsensual one at that. even when you say "here, take it back," they dont let you return it, even though you *are* the receipt. what are you to do? if the gender abolitionist project you are committed to is to eradicate the ravages of gender—which is, simply put, to say gender—how can you be about that life &, as they continue to demand of you, keep saying how much gender you have?

i know, i know. you & i both get it: insert social justice our-generation-wokeness here about privilege & all that. all that is very known. *but you need to understand . . .*, they say, though you understand quite well, but let them say that anyway because it is, after all, part of the ethical relation. you understand. & because you understand, when they tell you to *have* "male" privilege, they are telling you, to your abolitionist chagrin, to *have* masculinity. but youre out here trying to *slip between genders, shimmy past masculinity for a moment, but not really launch into another gender, trying to loft out of gender for a moment, compos-*

*ing some other body outside gender's gravity. To not-exist in a non-existing gender* . . . (thanks for this, McKenzie.)[6]

i gotta go,

X

X <x@undisclosedlocation.[dis]org> Wed Mar. 11, 2020 9:39 AM

To me

to whom it may concern:

maybe i'll see you later.

regards (or not),

X

# THE CO-ALITION OF GENDER ABOLITION

The first thing we've done is something without our consent (i.e. we're gendered). . . . I feel like [gender abolition] would look like . . . more space in our heads to think about something else. If people wanted to think about their bodies, they could still think about their bodies, but we could imagine ourselves without them. But I think it's hard. I often say that a world without this would mean we'd all stop looking at bodies and then we'd all stop looking at gender. I sometimes get the response, "But what about the people that want gender? Some people have fought for their gender and fought for their bodies so should be proud of it." So, I'm like, "Yes, but that's all still in relation to this world." If there was a world without gender expectations and stereotypes, I think these people would actually be like, "An arm, so what?" or "My stomach, so what?"—**Travis Alabanza,** *Trans Power*, 2019

I'm not so sure I "am," or if I must be, "want to be," any particular gender. They tell me, with clarity and verve, with the coercive function indexical of feminists old and misogynists new and old, that I—and all of us—*must* be, and *are*, men and women. To deem ourselves otherwise is an injustice. To deem ourselves otherwise is naïve, an attempted absolution.

It seems to me and my intellectual homies that the notion of identity, which is to say, y'all, an understanding of ourselves and others as beings who possess the property equivalent to the things we have been told we must, and can never not, be—this is the project of a philosophical tradition invested in, well, investment: a project invested in capital accumulation, in ownership, in exclusion, in immutability and its tethers fixing knowledge, not to mention cisnormative white supremacist heteropatriarchy (you *are* this thing that we tell you you are, a thing in hierarchical relation, a thing in mutually exclusionary relation). Identity, as we often understand and champion it, is the result of the carceral project of individuation, the name for individuation's nominalization, which makes then even the most idiosyncratically self-determined genders still seduced by its logics. So even when one comes up with a wholly self-formulated gender, it is still subject to language and concepts stemming from without—the, as it were, in Lordeian parlance, master's tools—and serves as an attempt to be an individual self, to break from relationality; to, in a real sense, become a sovereign, masterful subject—a master, a ruler, to have dominion over something even if it is oneself. Y'all who do not want the radicality of gender abolition, or something like it, have a bit of an obsession with power. Oh, no, no, no, that's not going to work for us. To the extent that identity disallows coalition and the kind of radical world to which we call out is the extent to which, precisely, exactly, we must forsake the identificatory project. Such a project prohibits, impedes, abolitionist strivings on the grounds that identity is the subjective instantiation, the coercively bestowed coveted possession, of the onto-epistemic project to which abolition stands as antithetical.

Gender abolition is about coalition for me; it is about a refusal of individuation, about coming together and knowing that we are already together. "Gender" as such does not allow for the kind of coming and being together in which I am interested, as underlying it is a violence of separation and exclusion, a violence of circumscription. And I don't want it. I don't want it, I don't want it. And, truthfully, I don't want you to want it either, because the wanting to want it is, I think, wanting to want a kind of carcerality and extrication from the sociality that engenders, possibly, radically other ways to be with one another. Gender abolition needs to occur now and it is deeply unsatisfactory to wait to do that when purportedly more important things are hashed out, especially not in service of some kind of ethics like "We can't get rid of gender right now or else how would we address gender-based harm?" Gender *is* the harm; what is sexism, discrimination, and assault along gendered lines but the *committing* of gender? We need not settle "woman" or even the parameters of "gender" in order to advance a politics in service of those harmed by sexism and, indeed, harmed by gender itself. *When laws and social policies represent women*, Judith Butler writes, reflecting on the legacy of their now thirty-year-old book, *they make tacit decisions about who counts as a woman, and very often make presuppositions about what a woman is. We have seen this in the domain of reproductive rights. So the question I was asking then is: do we need to have a settled idea of women, or of any gender, in order to advance feminist goals?*[1] And the answer, vociferously, is no. We can and have and should be doing subjectivity and sociality in ways that engender a different terrain on which we can live that need not, and perhaps should not, be concerned with a particular demographic. Not because that demographic does not matter but because it's less about the demographic and more, much more about the mechanisms in place—the histories, variable as they are; the discourses; the systems; the institutions, structures; the networks—that create demographic delimitations to be placed in hierarchical and antagonistic relationship. It is about what happened that made logical the invention of a denigrated class of people or nonpeople as natural. That is the cause, we must not forget. It's not like (and this is a contentious claim, to be sure) there were "women," categorically, and then it seemed natural to oppress them. The oppression *created* the class of women, not the other way around.

The ethical world we work toward is gotten to *by way of* abolishing gender; that world eradicates gender as such in its very course; we cannot wait to dissolve these divisions, these violent cuts to our sociality, inter- and intra-, after the revolution precisely because the process of moving toward this radical, just world involves, constitutively, tearing asunder gender.[2]

Coalition happens via nonsanctioned coming-togethers. That is, in excess of legible taxonomies and categorization—themselves imposed and given ontologies that exist ahead of us, that form us before we have a form or can choose a form or unform—coalition and radicality might more effectively arise through indiscrete, devious assemblages that do not map onto the state's grammars of demography. And gender is an impediment to our coming together, and oftentimes, if we do come together, a violent circumscription of *how* we are permitted to come together. Deemed a man and required to remain a man, to indeed be and do your manness, means that you cannot simply have platonic relationships with women. You cannot let that woman best you in this physical sport, or this game of wits; you cannot let her, in any way, "control" you or have you on a leash or "whipped"; you cannot work together with her without there being the possibility of sexual exchange; you cannot interact with her on nonviolent grounds. You cannot not do gender with her. You cannot not do gender with anyone.

How can we, truly, come together with this in place?

Coalition is not, to my mind, to be conflated with community; it is to stave off such co-optations as different colored hands holding one another or differently gendered people being chummy; it is to stave off prideful rainbows, not least of which is because the city in which I live can proudly sport rainbow decals on its cop cars. I am quite thoroughly bored by calls for community that have as their fundamental aim the cobbling together of quote-unquote diverse peoples in service of representative optics that ultimately obscure the violence of needing to be known and thus curtailed in order to participate in struggle, the violence of representational optics that monolithize and disallow generative dissent within a purportedly discrete sector of a grid, the violence, indeed, of a categoricality that coaxed them together as categorically different. What interests me is a coalitional groove—rubbing associations, Rod Ferguson might call this—wherein we come together, revise what and how we mean in that coming together, mutate into an assemblage, temporary as it may be, that engenders a certain kind of force or politicality not predicated on subjective discretion. Not predicated on being this kind of subject, through and through.

The traditions that have forged me, a black radical one and a trans insurgent one, make indiscretion a generative imperative. From my vantage, black radicality is an accretion that has gifted the thinking that a subversive relation to power foundations one's subjective inhabitation of the world, while trans insurgency is expressive of an ineffable and corporeally irreverent torquing of the criteria for meaning-making that gestures like t4t mobilize across and in excess of taxonomies to ensure survivability, never presupposing or predicating this mobilization on identitarian or subjective sameness. All of this is to say that I am loved by, and thus try to proliferate, not radical inclusivity but radical nonexclusivity. Coalition's nonexclusivity means that we cast no one out, that no one is disposable, that in the rubbing and generative friction in the work is the always present possibility of one being changed, radically, by the rubbing and friction.

*I WANT TO BELONG SOMEWHERE*, McKenzie Wark says in a trans gesture that reckons with how her transness necessitates, in some way, the obliteration of what has become the being onto which her transness is cast, *but I don't want an identity*.[3] The very notion of "identity" is a bad philosophical project that has held sovereign sway over how we've understood what is possible for us. There is an obsession with how to pin down, how to get at the fundamental element, how to not have to think about being something else at the heart of the Westphalian international order, this political and philosophical project of sovereignty. We can be without making recourse to the paltry scraps we've been given like a bad flight offering only chicken or fish when we've been vegans for a while now. What would it be like to have food that sustains us, food we can eat, food that is not predicated on the slaughtering of others?

Identity is not irrelevant since irrelevance would slyly imply a consideration and a decision against further consideration. No, identity is nulled here. It makes of those to whom it is said to apply artifacts that arrive onto the scene only insofar as they stay confined within the bounds of the identity whose criteria are always wrapped in the garb of language not of one's own making. Identity as an apparatus of legibilizing, of interpellating, requires that those for whom the identity is definitional only *be* inasmuch as they measure up to the identity and, most crucially, do not permit themselves to be other than the identity which commits an atrocious monopolizing of how one can emerge as a subject.

Let me double back and take another route, one more scenic: there is an immeasurable array of wondrous ways I might have come into the world, which is not to say that my physiognomy is infinitely mutable but that my physiognomy is always subject to being read, a reading that is vastly contingent on what is discursively and historically permissible, which claims the very meaning, the very contour, of me-as-existent. To be given an identity, which is always the causal relation, for we are thrown into a terrain we are forced to struggle with, is to be disallowed, from the jump, the other things in the array of possibilities. It is because identity is invoked as an immutable possession—what we simply are, obscuring its construction. Identity, put bluntly, is a project of promoting subjective purity for the sake of being corralled into machinic grease for the systems in place that wish only for their own perpetuation.

So I promote abolition of one of the vectors of identity: gender. Which is to say, *it's an abolition of sovereignty. It's an abolition of a certain hor-*

*rible and brutal individuated notion of freedom. And it's an abolition of the world that is constructed on that conceptual framework.*[4]

It may not be about erecting something at all. It may be much more fruitful, and interesting, to think of how we can come to something like what we might have been through gender abolition. Through, as it were, a project not of putting things together but of viewing with soft eyes, feeling with humbled breath, the gloriousness of how things fall apart. In the shards lying there is a mosaic of pieces you can pick up and carry with you, fondling it in your hands, tucking it in your pocket, only to discard it later; or you can stomp on the shards, grinding them into smaller pieces, awing at their disintegration; or, further still, you can step over the pile, walking into the sunset.

WHEN IT COMES to abolition, something I have attempted to broach with the kindness and timidity indicative of the radical and tenacious worldview from which it stems, it seems to me that its radicality is precisely its gift. Its radicality is the very thing often hampering it from assuming a pervasiveness, and yet, ironically, it is the very thing that, if made pervasive, might alleviate the anxieties that seem to foreclose its generative possibility, its realization. Abolition emerges as a prophetic force, as it were, but like many prophets is castigated in its own time for refusing the system that must be refused. Calling out and demanding the departure from an abusive lover, abolition is maligned as hating love.

The abolition of gender, as a call, is, for me, a hesitation. Staccato life away from this lashed-on somatic meaning I never asked for and do not want. There is radicality in the desire for the utterly overturned like the tables in the temple after the outburst of that divine citizen of Nazareth (gender as the very den for all those robbers), to be sure, but there is, too, timidity, tinkering along the way, hesitation at certain turns for cautionary purposes so as to preserve and proliferate as much life as possible. It is wrongly characterized—gender abolition, that is—as the homogenization of the masses. It is wrongly characterized as turning away from power relations invoked in histories and structures that buttress the validity of some bodily comportments over others. And it is wrongly characterized as the "agenda" of those who wish to rebuke the axioms of biology. Y'all don't hear me: gender abolition, for those in the back, the front, and the side, does not claim to require homogeneity, the absolution of privileges bestowed on certain bodily comportments (which, I must make clear, is not to say one's gender, is not to concede gender identification to external perceptions of one's body), or biologically evaluative evacuation. We must say this, and keep saying it, or else we will continue to be woefully misunderstood and, at worst, written off violently.

(Y'all still not hearing me, it seems. It's like: my uncle—my mother's only brother—has been incarcerated for over twenty-five years. Since I was, like, four years old or something. I remember photos and photos of my growing body and varying hairstyles—fade, braids, locs, back to fade, fro—with my uncle and my mom and my brother. And I remember the photos my uncle would send us of him and his friends, brown jumpsuits, always one or two in the front of the group, squatting down, likely with a peace sign up. He has detailed to me all the ways being locked up has propounded violences. Sexual assaults, constant surveillance, the utter deprivation of privacy, malnutritional diets needing to be supplemented by family and friends' money to buy more than the slop served in the mess hall. [And be it forbidden if the prison goes on lockdown, in which case you get a bologna sandwich, an apple, and a bottle of water for each meal.] These are the conditions on which incarceration is founded. They are conditions, wholly and without qualification, of violence. There is another thing in our midst that behaves similarly [which is not to say exactly the same]. A thing that requires constant surveillance, policing of its boundaries, what to wear and with whom to converse, reprimand if done incorrectly or if smuggling in something improper to its realm, imagistic perpetuation of itself, what to consume, where to go, whom to love, and dismally limited options. Thus: gender itself is a kind of prison. What is needed is defiance of this system, which is, more accurately, a system inasmuch as the prison industrial complex is enabled, in part, by gender normativity; *regimes of normative sexuality and gender*, that is, *are organizing structures of the prison industrial complex*. Gender as such is a product and producer of carceral logics; the surveillance query "Are you a boy or a girl?" and the admonition that "Boys don't do that" are disciplinary behaviors indexical of carcerality. Thus, abolition entails the *radical deconstruction* of heteronormativity, the gender binary, and all their attending vectors. Gender must be abolished.)[5]

Gender abolition, you see, is a move toward something like freedom.

THERE ARE OBJECTIONS, of course. There are those who have castigated gender abolition as a super-white fantasy inattentive to the effects of racialization on gender, and indeed the love, say, a black woman might have of her gender. How dare the gender abolitionist say that we should abolish gender when the black woman (on the assumption, usually, that they are cisgender and have the capacity to house a fetus) finally begins to understand the gifts of her capacity as more than a damnation to birthing chattel? How dare the gender abolitionist say that we should abolish gender when there are black women loving black women primarily on the grounds that they are black women? And these, I assure you, are quite serious accusations, accusations that cannot, must not, be waved off as uninformed. These accusations require that we tarry with the discomfiture they lay bare.

The meditation here requires deep care. Of the critical variety, one of the most pervasive rationales for rejecting gender abolition is that it does not allow for a critical encounter with power relations—gender abolition, it goes, flattens gender differentiation, making impossible addressing social positionings based on gender. Put differently, how can you address the structural inequities of women in the workforce if, following gender abolition, there are no "women"? Posed as a response to gender abolition is a humbler gender *democratization*, where gender is not dissolved into nothingness—a misnomeric reading of abolition which I shall get to in due time, don't you worry—but committed to equalizing the gender order. Democratizing genders does not shrink gender but pluralizes it, understood as more favorable on the grounds that genders allow people to know how they are situated in the world. Democratizing gender also concedes in a very real, very fundamental sense, that gender is, has always been, and should always be a way of calculating the body. Your gender, whatever it is, is valid, and your lived experience attests to its validity, which, for that very reason, makes it something that we should never, ever rid ourselves of.

Others tout gender abolition as—and I am not overstating the professed claim here—colonization. As many of those who advocate for gender abolition are white, there is the thought that because of this the conceptual framework propelling it is an extension of colonization efforts to proliferate whiteness. (I suppose that I, then, am an aberration, brainwashed perhaps, or, as my incarcerated students have grown to love as a catchall for anything they deem nonblack that black people do, "self-hate.") To say that gender is socially constructed is to deprive it of its staying power, but it remains a power that is historically variable in its constancy. We, societally, have placed importance in gender, have given it a category, have held it dear to us over centuries. If we then go out evangelizing the abolition of gender we are intervening in worlds and cultures we ought not to and spreading the doctrine of a troublesome creed. Writes Lola Phoenix in a piece titled "Gender Abolition as Colonisation,"

> The problem with abolishing gender is that not only do we have to define it, apply our definition towards other cultures, demand they remove gender from their own race, cultural, spiritual or whatever background, but also assume that the abolition of the concept of gender will result in equality or a lack of discrimina-

tion. In doing so, from a white perspective, we effectively create a colonising project wherein we're intervening in their own identities, behaviours, and practices in an attempt to make their lives better.[6]

I've gone through a few reactions reading this: a furrowing of my brow, chuckling, shaking my head, rolling my eyes. First (or *first of all*), we do not, in fact, have to define abolition, which belies its open-endedness, an open-endedness that shuttles in its most potent efficacy. It is the impulse to define, definitively, once and for all, that got us into this gendered mess. What is gender itself, in fact, but a treacherous, insistent will to define, applying that definition throughout the world and punishing those who fall outside of that definition? Abolition, contrastingly, is an undefinitional project, an attempt to undefine, radically, toward no definition. Second, it does not necessitate that we cast our abolitionist net globally, demanding other cultures do the same. Surely, we might understand gender abolition as the move to make, but we are not demanding that all cultures across the globe take up the task as well because we know, trust, that not only is that not a good look historically but also that other cultures are way further ahead of us in this respect—there are some cultures out there that are already in gender abolitionist territory. Third, thoroughgoing gender abolition would very well result in a more equitable (not *equal*) and just relationality precisely because such an abolition would not simply be not talking about gender—which it seems you, and others, assume—but rather the eradication of the vectors and footholds endowed with a meaning from which gender discriminatory differentials could be extracted. It appears you equate it with shutting our eyes, covering our ears, and screaming *La, la, la, I'm not listening!*; but we, on the other hand, seek a more radical project: the deprivation of gender that touts itself Gender as an extractive vector hierarchizing our relation to others and the world. Fourth, if intervening means that we necessitate the eradication of genders that emerge through the denigration, wholesale, of other, subordinated genders and requisite violation of others in order to buttress itself, then so be it. That is, yes, intervene in the dude buttressing his masculinity—*his* gender—by beating his girlfriend. Intervene every time.

Contra gender abolition, everyone's gender is A-OK "as long as it doesn't hurt anyone," everyone's gender is "valid," everyone's understanding of (their) gender is totally cool because it's their "lived experience," and all this, at some point in my life, seemed pristinely sensible. I fully championed it. I do not wish to commit violence to y'all, because I know it is all in the interest of mitigating gendered harm. Speak of me not in hushed tones of hostility, please, for I, too, wish to mitigate the harm, though I know some might accuse me precisely of the inverse. I need to push back on the prevailing discourse in the circles I traverse only because there is sedimenting within them a troubling liberalism manifesting as incessant uncriticality. Such a pervasive liberalism, which is not to say radicalism or leftism, *is mostly just an appeal to maintain the status quo, since "hurting others" gets defined as doing anything that upsets the privileged class*, a manner of engagement that cannot make sense of the kind of trans radicalism we seek.[7] The categories, whatever they are, are always good, yes-yes-yes, because you say your experience has been such that you have a sense of yourself thanks to gender. Don't you dare take that away from me.

But most of us know full well that we often love the names we are called because, by a masterful feat and collective struggle, we have come to be okay with naming ourselves by those names. I disagree not at all that those names can be a home for us. It seems to me that the naming itself, the impulse to attribute names, is what goes unaddressed.

: : :

A conversation I had with a colleague, one of the most radically ethical and ethically radical scholars I know: it was conveyed to me that, when speaking to one of their partners, their nesting partner, there was the assertion that it is not so much that gender itself is bad but gender *roles*. Launching from the generative phrase, riffing on a few mutually loved queer theorists, that gender might be a kind of prison, the two of them came to a tentative consensus that gender is not imprisoning but that gender roles, the forcing of certain kinds of gendered behaviors, is what is imprisoning. They both agreed that there was much that was limiting about gender; they conceded its restrictiveness. But my colleague was forced to pause when thinking about trans people who find liberation in gender when they are able to articulate their gender identity in contradistinction to their birth-assigned gender-prison. At least the way it is articulated by friends, gender is a kind of prison at one time and a kind of liberation at another. And I don't want to erase that reality for many people. My colleague's partner—also a phenomenally lovely and erudite person—noted that the problem is that there is a conception of one, singular thing called masculinity that is really about gender roles rather than gender itself. For their partner, no two people have *the same* gender, and thus gender is infinite in its expressions by individuals. So now, my colleague wrote, "I'm wondering about how to disarticulate gender from *gender roles* and what this might have to do with thinking about abolition and queer liberation."

I was invited to respond, and I did, thankful for such a carefully thought through exchange. My response: Is it "proper" to say that trans folks who move away from birth-assigned genders and find "liberation" in, say, womanhood, as trans women are indeed liberated? That is, might it still be accurate to say that gender is *a kind of* prison in this scenario? Because, from my perspective, both genders—the assigned one and the chosen one—are *different* prisons, though one is more capacious and comfortable than the other. I am uninterested in more roomy, responsive, lusher prisons; even the trans woman's gender is such that it couldn't not be chosen, that is, the possibility to not be a gender, to be something other-than a gender, is always and already foreclosed. And that is the carcerality inherent to gender as such: one cannot become outside of gender; it is coercive and compulsory. This is not to denigrate the chosen prison, as it were; however, I am still hesitant to clap for the trans woman's "liberation" if she chooses a differently textured womanhood, which has, as we know, a history of a whole bunch of violence that might be described as imprisoning. It is that gender demands knowledge of us, from us, and about us. There is an invasive needing to know that gender dictates; or, one *must be* a gender, and a proper one, and this becomes requisite knowledge for the very possibility of engaging another. In short, I need to know not simply what your gender is, but that *you are gendered*, and you cannot interact with me until those grounds are settled.

Too, I also wonder if inherent to gender *is* gender role. I'm genuinely uncertain about whether gender is possible without gender roles, if gender as an expression and identity is inextricable from a given role. Can, say, masculinity exist without having to do masculinity, where "masculinity's" meaning is up for debate, I suppose, yet still carries the baggage of toxicity? I come, thus, to this thought: this is a question of subjectivity for me. Subjectivity happens as one is interpellated into categories that are hegemonically deemed legible, which is to say that subjectivity itself—the extent to which one appears—is given ahead of the subject that is formed. Which is to say, differently, one is imprisoned *in order to appear*. If gender is one of the more fundamental aspects of subjectivity, the extent to which we appear as legible gendered subjects might mean the extent to which we imprison ourselves to be seen. And that's messed up.

We have all this discourse on policing as deleterious to the well-being of our communities, and as radical abolitionists we demand the end of policing, right? If we are to live this assertion, to really be about that life, it is crucial to heed an ameliorative and abolitionist politics toward the ways that gender is policed, which is not merely the ways certain genders are derogated over or against others that are permitted sovereign sway, but more the ways gender itself functions as an extension, an iteration, of policing. Knowing this, we got work to do, y'all—namely, we are to *avoid at all cost the danger of . . . helping the existing cops and judges by becoming a snitch*. Or when we see illegible genders flourishing or various departures from the gender binary, we are not to snitch on those genders; indeed, we are to engage the philosophical radicality of gender abolition by *lend[ing] an ear to the signal, rather than rushing to the police station.*[8] The chants for no cops and no prisons includes the gender police and gendered imprisonment, too. And since gender is an imposition, a nonconsensual, required imposition we are punished for not receiving on the terms of the imposition, which puts gender in the realm of the transitive verb—*to gender*; *gendering*—then gender abolition would just as readily urge an antigender disposition as it would urge, like many already do, an antiracist and anticapitalist disposition.

It's like, what is a gender that is not ascribed certain roles? Is not the very process of gendering, be it from within or without, a requirement to adhere to the roles, the structure, that support its very definition? Gender cannot be what it is, I do not think, without its enforceability. Gender as such, its whole deal, is an imposed inscription that makes certain demands of its subject. As a legibilizing categorization, gender is not so cute and innocent as a description or noble and just an acknowledgment of difference. Rather, from the radical purview of the many-handed hunger of trans radicality, (gender) categorization is difference's enforcement, *keep[ing] things apart that could well be together.* Gender abolition is the abolition of the enforcement of categorization, the enforcement embedded in categorization as an impulse—that is, taxonomic gender, which is to say gender as such. Gender abolition foregrounds, world-builds, a yearning *to belong and yet be free of category.*[9] While the dust still swarms after the abolition, because it will not settle, the look and feel of gender abolition is not homogeneity but a promiscuous togetherness in singular sociality.

That gender is constitutive of subjectivity, and that subjectivity as an adherence to the mandates that permit one to appear onto the scene of legible sociality is compulsory, means that gender is always, definitionally, laden with demands that are never innocent or neutral. Thus, to advocate for gender abolition is to refuse reformist gestures such as broadening the juridical ambit to include transgender people or accommodate changes in sex designation on identification documents; acceptance of different pronouns than that which one might "expect"; or deeming anyone's gender expression "valid." These ultimately serve the legitimation of gender as a necessary apparatus of social organization, overlooking the violence in the necessity itself, the circumscription in disallowing other modes of life that exceed gender. These maneuvers serve as the foundation of the very possibility of subjectivity with a requisite gender legibility that meets established criteria for entry into sociality. Our salvation might then be a radical obsession with not being a subject, as the surety of being—finding, incessantly, what gender one is and knowing, factually, that one and others are this gender over that gender rather than imagining the possibility of not having to be a gender, to do and relate to others on gender's terms, at all—emerges as much less useful and loving than the constant interrogation of being; to abandon subjectivity, constitutive of which is gender, as the onto-metaphysical ligaments of being are major impediments to the radical freedom those of us committed to insurrectionary ethics, might be our best bet. There is indeed something so beautiful about refusing one's assignation, a beauty made beautiful in that one's assignment is the quelling of imaginative possibilities not yet dreamed or felt or thought or lived by the subject who could not have existed but for the foreclosure of that imagination. So we seek what black feminist abolitionist Miriam Kaba calls a *jailbreak of the imagination*, where unrestrained and unfettered, radically nonpunitive and nonwounding, life is moved toward by way of the eradication of "bad" genders, sure, but more fundamentally the creation of a world where we can be with ourselves and others unviolated.[10]

THE CONDITION FOR FREEDOM to constitute our emergence with and through one another is one in which we give up knowledge of the other. The playful jest my grandmother would offer, when I'd return home from college for holidays, running to give her a hug as she sat in her chair—because she does not get up for you; you come to her—bubbles up as a loving "Who you? Do I know you?" She'd shift quickly to a grinning "How you doin', baby?" because no matter how old I get,

I will always be her baby, her usurping my mother for ownership of my natality. But the "Do I know you?," with its playful love, conditions another way of knowing, conditions a way of knowing her "baby" anew, on terms not ceded to the past and believed to be teleological or static. She loves me through, albeit briefly, not knowing me. The babying could be quite intentional, my grandmother wishing for me a nubility hefty with possibility and unpredetermined avenues. She babies me upon each of these occasions not to infantilize me but to permit my rebirthing, unbeholden to sedimented grammars.

And this is significant, I want to say. It founds another way of loving not requiring capturative knowledge of someone or something in its entirety. Love can arise in, precisely, the not knowing. And this extends outward, for me at least, to the very people who are not, will never be, *my* "baby."

Approaching strangers, acknowledging them and speaking of them, as I've said before to many folks in my life, presents me with an ethical imperative. Each time; no exceptions, ideally, though I surely fail over and over. The ethical imperative is, if the Bard had been in a class or two of mine or had read a little bit of queer theory, *To gender, or not to gender? That is the question.* . . . If seeing gender as a regulative, external imposition has any merit, it requires of us, then, that we refuse its regulation, one that is nonconsensual. Something as seemingly innocuous as "I like that man's shirt" imposes an entire archive of experiences, histories, expectations, bodily demands, and relations to others that can only be read as a fundamental violence. Gender works to reveal that which is hidden and presumed to be the "real" site of one's supposed sex, which would mark the validity or fallaciousness of the gender being presented—or, more closely, the gender being read and inscribed with a noninnocent meaning. There is no right to privacy, and no critical apparatus as to the cogency of the inscriptions being made. The read presentation is made to coax what is supposed to be going on downstairs, and in this way the process of gendering, the act of giving, forcefully, one a gender by way of the heavily mediated process of inscribing gendered meaning onto another filtered through, often times, the violence of the gender binary, is, as Talia Bettcher claims, *inherently abusive*: *gender presentation is taken to communicate genital status*, and thus *it compels euphemistic disclosures of intimate information.*[11] Your "I like that man's shirt," I am telling you, is not just an offhand comment, a comment by which nothing is meant. When I share this with you, please know that I am only trying, in small and large ways, to allow others to live more fully. It is an attempt for nonviolated life, a violation of which gender and its enforcement—because gender as such *is* an enforcement, an embodied rule we are required to live by and thus required to have forced upon us and others—is a prime suspect.

It is easy enough to see that the binary and perinatal assignations are impositions, nonconsensually given identities that work overwhelmingly to the harm of oneself and others inasmuch as that violation is the trauma through which one is permitted to exist in the world. So ask me not who I am, what my gender *is*; and ask me not to verify others'. That is the work of the police, and if we are to aspire toward police abolition, toward no new (or old) jails, it seems to me we are required to take our claims to their end: the abolition of gender. This livable wreckage is where, in a Foucauldian sense, *it's not the assertion of identity that's important.*[12] It is where, in Dora Silva Santana's sense, a Santanaian sense, as it were, we are constituted by *a movement of liberation against gendered racialized oppression*, it is *moving across and along the waters, the imposed limits of gender.*[13] There is another way, are other ways, to live in this world that exhaust the arrangements in place.

# NOTES

PREFACE

1. Keegan, *Lana and Lilly Wachowski*, 46. Emphasis in original.

2. Keegan, *Lana and Lilly Wachowski*, 46. I must also note that my operative term has been utilized in a similar, though still different, context. Viviane Vergueiro's thesis "Por inflexões decoloniais de corpos e identidades de gênero inconformes: uma análise autoetnográfica da cisgeneridade como normatividade," drawing on decolonial thought and world-systems analysis, reads:

> I use "world-cystem" in reference to Grosfoguel (2012, 339), who characterizes a "Westernized, christianity-centric, modern, colonial, capitalist, patriarchal world [c]ystem" that produces "epistemic hierarchies" that—according to the specific reading that this thesis offers—exclude, minimize, or silence non-cisgender perspectives. The grammatically corrupted "cystem," like other, similar corrruptions, has the objective of emphasizing the structural and institutional character—the "cystemic"—of cis-sexist perspectives, to move beyond the individualizing paradigm of the "transphobia" concept. (15; translated from Portuguese by my partner: thank you ☺)

3. Chen, *Trans Exploits*, 96; Richardson, *Queer Limit of Black Memory*, 7.

4. Salamon, *Assuming a Body*, 1.

5. Detournay, "Racial Life of 'Cisgender,'" 60; Krell, "Is Transmisogyny Killing Trans Women of Color?," 234; Chen, *Trans Exploits*, 98; Spillers, "Mama's Baby, Papa's Maybe," 80; Rosenberg, *Confessions of the Fox*, 296.

BACK IN THE DAY

1. First italicized portion from Beanie Sigel, "Remember Them Days," 2000; second italicized portion from Psalm One (ft. Manic Focus), "Joy in the Noise," 2017.

2. Awkward-Rich, "Trans, Feminism," 833.

3. The italics in this and the two preceding paragraphs come from Halberstam, "Unbuilding Gender." Emphasis added.

4. Blanchard, "In Defense of the Trans Villainess."

5. Italicized portions from Warren, "Calling into Being," 271.

6. Italicized portions from Stein, *Avidly Reads*, 70.

7. I say this tongue in cheek, of course. I don't *really* mean this.

Actually, yeah, I do mean this. The blackest, hands down.

8. "Fusion Gems," Steven Universe Wiki, https://steven-universe.fandom.com/wiki/Fusion_Gems (accessed September 3, 2021).

9. "Don't you put that evil on me, Ricky Bobby! Don't you put that on us!" *Talladega Nights: The Ballad of Ricky Bobby*, dir. Adam McKay (Columbia Pictures, 2006).

10. Italicized portions from Emi Koyama "Frequently Asked Questions: Basic Information," Eminism.org, https://eminism.org/faq/basic.html (accessed September 3, 2021).

11. Italicized portions from Tourmaline, Stanley, and Burton, *Trap Door*, xviii.

12. Mock, *Redefining Realness*, 16.

13. Italicized portions from Seymour, "None Shall Pass."

14. Rosenberg, *Confessions of the Fox*, xii.

HEART OF CISNESS

1. Malcolm X, "The Ballot or the Bullet," King Solomon Baptist Church, Detroit, Michigan, April 12, 1964, http://americanradioworks.publicradio.org/features/blackspeech/mx.html.

2. ross, "Call It What It Is."

3. Ziyad, "My Gender Is Black." The quote in the sentence preceding the block quote here is from Joshua Chambers-Letson, *After the Party: A Manifesto for Queer of Color Life* (New York: NYU Press, 2018), xiv.

4. Spillers, "Mama's Baby, Papa's Maybe," 77, emphasis in original; "trans to gender" is from Warren, "Calling into Being," 271.

5. Chaudhry, "Trans/Coalitional Love-Politics," 530, 535. Chaudhry notes that in the field "there is, as yet, limited scholarship attending to how cisgender has emerged and been taken up institutionally in opposition to transgender"—a very astute observation (522). This very book is an attempt to put forth that scholarship.

6. Snorton, *Black on Both Sides*, 7, 2.

7. Snorton, *Black on Both Sides*, 136.

8. Crawley, "Stayed | Freedom | Hallelujah," 29.

9. Moten, *Stolen Life*, xii.

10. Moten, *Stolen Life*, x.

11. In Iowa on October 26, 2019, a fifty-six-year-old woman was killed by flying debris after a gender reveal explosion. On September 5, 2020, a family set off pyrotechnics to spectacularize their gender reveal party in El Dorado Ranch Park in California, subsequently scorching over 7,000 acres in two days. On April 23, 2017, a Border Patrol agent ignited a massive wildfire during a gender reveal party that burned through 47,000 acres of Arizona grasslands, costing more than $8 million and taking two weeks to extinguish. "Gender reveals" traffic in a slew of fucked-up notions of gender expectations, essentialism, biological determinism, and hegemonic and normative yuck-worthy nonsense ("Rifles or Ruffles?" was one gender reveal set of options; "Stick or No Stick? another; and "Pistols or Pearls?" another). On the one hand, there's a super lukewarm critique, a critique more about a boomer technophobia than the genderiness of the gender reveals themselves—"'What was once a joyous moment shared between mother and father has become a spectacle for all to ogle at' goes the refrain, romanticizing a past that never was in the effort to pin all moral decay on androids and iPads," writes Rae Gray. "Casting these parties as some kind of modern trend when they are anything but. Gender-reveal parties are a public version of the father in the waiting room handing out cigars—and that's kinda the point." They are, more fundamentally, a reinforcement of the gender binary, Gray notes. But, yo, even more than that, this shit is *deadly*. The explosions and deaths only dramatize the slow deaths and internal conflagrations that happen when people cannot not be the narrow confines placed upon them. The anguish to have to have the "stick" and brandish the stick, to have the biggest stick, to be defective and punish-worthy if not doing what one ought to do with the stick; to cock that "pistol" and do what pistols are meant to do: kill, harm, intimidate, threaten; to be defined by lack, having no stick but good try, here's a consolation prize: someone with a stick; to be defined by glittery jewels and literally commodified. How utterly violent. Gray, "Pistols or Pearls."

12. Riley, *Am I That Name?*, 2.

13. Butler, *Bodies That Matter*, xv. Emphasis in original.

14. Critchley, "Being and Time."

15. Zadjermann, dir., *Judith Butler*.

16. Briggs, "These Are Not My People."

17. Italicized portions from Seymour, "None Shall Pass."

18. Scheman, *Shifting Ground*, 144.

19. Butler, "Conscience Doth Make Subjects," 25.

HOW YA MAMA'N'EM?

An earlier version of this essay, "How Ya Mama'n'em? Blackness, Nonbinariness, and Radical Subjectivity," appeared in *Peitho: Journal of the Coalition of Feminist Scholars in the History of Rhetoric and Composition* 22, no. 4 (Summer 2020): n.p.

1. Passages found in Bjorkman, "Singular *They*," 80.

2. Hess, "Who's 'They'?"; Weber, "Leslie Feinberg."

3. Rajunov and Duane, eds., *Nonbinary*, 48–49.

4. Italicized portions from Moten, "Come On, Get It!"

5. I take this term from J. Kameron Carter, who used it as a way to escape the teleologics of whiteness, as a nega-taxonomizing gesture, at the Black Theology and Black Power Conference at Northwestern University on November 1, 2019.

6. Da Silva, *Toward a Global Idea of Race*, xviii–ix.

7. Italicized portions from Detournay, "Racial Life of 'Cisgender,'" 66. See also Krell, "Is Transmisogyny Killing Trans Women of Color?," 232.

8. Italicized portion from Kelley and Moten, "Do Black Lives Matter?"

9. Italicized portions from King, *Black Shoals*, 73.

10. Huxtable, *Mucous in My Pineal Gland*, 12. Capitalization in original.

11. Quote from "Good Light" in Gibson', *Lord of the Butterflies*, 20.

12. I've taken this from one of Nat Raha's Facebook statuses. Brackets in original.

13. Rajunov and Duane, *Nonbinary*, 76. Emphasis added.

NOTES ON (TRANS)GENDER

1. Bettcher, "Trapped in the Wrong Theory," 394.

2. Italicized portion from Hayward, "More Lessons from a Starfish," 66.

3. Halberstam, *Trans**, 4.

4. Stryker, "Transgender Issue," 149.

5. Snorton, *Black on Both Sides*, 2.

6. Italicized portions from Snorton, *Black on Both Sides*, 24, 33.

7. Beauchamp, *Going Stealth*, 82–83.

8. Collins, *Black Feminist Thought*, 11.

9. Devereaux, "Rollersets and Realness."

10. Italicized portions from Moten, *Stolen Life*, x.

11. Italicized portions from Malatino, *Trans Care*, 11.

12. Italicized portions from Enke, *Transfeminist Perspectives*, 73. Emphasis in original.

13. Krell, "Is Transmisogyny Killing Trans Women of Color?," 235.

14. An interesting little tidbit: the OED, as one of the references for the word *cis*, cites Thomas Jefferson, who wrote, "Our second maxim [should be], never

to suffer Europe to intermeddle with cis-Atlantic affairs." Here there is a solid thread of connection between *cis* and the sovereign force of nation-building, establishing bordered identities, and demarcating this side, the cis side, in contradistinction from the other side, the former positively and the latter negatively connoted. What is more, though, is the use of the Atlantic. The Atlantic, that oceanic middle leg of the transatlantic slave trade, is potent with racialized meaning, potent with the black flesh lying in remnants on the floor like the saline-saturated effluvium of unwanted, or unruly, or rebellious, waste. This racialized thread concatenates with the gendered specter haunting Jefferson's use of *cis*, a thread strung through the Atlantic—an effluvial hydraulic terrain which we must never forget to syntactically render as "the black Atlantic has always been a queer Atlantic," which means, too, that the black Atlantic has always been that *evil twin* of the Atlantic's queerness: the *trans*. Tinsley, "Black Atlantic, Queer Atlantic," 191; see also Stryker, "Transgender Studies," 212–15.

15. Italicized portion from Moten, "Black Op," 1746.

16. Green, "Essential I/Eye in We," 196. Emphasis in original.

17. Italicized portion from Stryker, Currah, and Moore, "Introduction," 13.

18. Stryker and Whittle, *Transgender Studies Reader*, 8.

19. Italicized portions from Martel, *Misinterpellated Subject*, 266.

20. Roche, *Trans Power*, 14.

21. Italicized portions from Wilchins, *Read My Lips*, 127.

22. Wilchins, *TRANS/Gressive*, 19.

23. Italicized portions from Wilchins, *Read My Lips*, 200, 206.

## BLOWING UP NARNIA

1. Barthes, *Neutral*, 41. Emphasis in original.

2. First italicized portion from Solanas, *SCUM Manifesto*; second italicized portion from Halberstam, *Queer Art of Failure*, 4.

3. Brand, *Blue Clerk*, 18.

4. Inspired by Thom, *Fierce Femmes and Notorious Liars*.

5. Detournay, "Racial Life of 'Cisgender,'" 62.

6. The Jacksons, "Blame It on the Boogie," Track 1 on *Destiny*, Epic-CBS, 1978:

> Don't blame it on the sunshine
> Don't blame it on the moonlight
> Don't blame it on the good times
> Blame it on the boogie.

7. Italicized portions from Carter, *Race*, 30; and Carter, "Black Malpractice," 69.

8. See Horton-Stallings, *Funk the Erotic*.

9. Sexton, *Black Men, Black Feminism*. All subsequent references will be given in parentheticals.

10. Hardt and Negri, *Assembly*, xxi.

11. Hayward and Gossett, "Impossibility of That," 18.

12. Italicized portions from Henderson, "Becoming Lesbian," 186.

RE: [NO SUBJECT]

An earlier version of this essay appeared under the title "RE: [No Subject]—On Nonbinary Gender," in *Qui Parle: Critical Humanities and Social Sciences* 30, no. 2 (2021): 229–47.

1. Wilchins, *Read My Lips*, 127.

2. Wilchins, *Read My Lips*, 96.

3. Green, "Race and Gender Are Not the Same!"

4. Salamon, "Place Where Life Hides Away," 96.

5. Nelson, *Argonauts*, 52–53.

6. Wark, *Reverse Cowgirl*, 96.

THE COALITION OF GENDER ABOLITION

1. Ferber, "Judith Butler on the Culture Wars."

2. See Gonzalez, "Communization and the Abolition of Gender." Gonzalez writes, and this is what I am riffing on, "It is no longer possible to imagine a situation in which social divisions are dissolved *after* the revolution"; "gender must be torn asunder in the process of the revolution"; "in order to be revolution at all, communization must destroy gender *in its very course*."

3. Wark, "Many-Handed Hunger of Transsexuality."

4. Moten, "Ensemble."

5. Italicized portions from Stanley and Smith, eds., *Captive Genders*, 4–8.

6. Phoenix, "Gender Abolition as Colonisation."

7. Thom, *I Hope We Choose Love*, 27.

8. Italicized portions from Badiou, *Can Politics Be Thought?*, 11.

9. Italicized portions from Wark, "Many-Handed Hunger of Transsexuality."

10. Kaba, "Jailbreak of the Imagination."

11. Bettcher and Goulimari, "Theorizing Closeness," 51.

12. Quoted in Zurn, "Politics of Anonymity," 28.

13. Santana, "Transitionings and Returnings," 183.

# BIBLIOGRAPHY

Alabanza, Travis. "Travis Alabanza." In *Trans Power*, edited by Juno Roche, 47–70. London: Jessica Kingsley, 2019.

Awkward-Rich, Cameron. "Trans, Feminism: Or, Reading like a Depressed Transsexual." *Signs: Journal of Women in Culture and Society* 42, no. 4 (2017): 819–41.

Bacon, Francis. *Of Vicissitudes of Things*. Whitefish, MT: Kessinger, 2010.

Badiou, Alain. *Can Politics Be Thought?* Translated by Bruno Bosteels. Durham, NC: Duke University Press, 2018.

Barthes, Roland. *The Neutral: Lecture Course at the Collège de France, 1977–1978*. Translated by Thomas Clerc and Eric Marty. New York: Columbia University Press, 2005.

Beauchamp, Toby. *Going Stealth: Transgender Politics and U.S. Surveillance Practices*. Durham, NC: Duke University Press, 2019.

Bettcher, Talia Mae. "Trapped in the Wrong Theory: Rethinking Trans Oppression and Resistance." *Signs: Journal of Women in Culture and Society* 39, no. 2 (Winter 2014): 383–406.

Bettcher, Talia, and Pelagia Goulimari. "Theorizing Closeness: A Trans Feminist Conversation." *Angelaki* 22, no. 1 (2017): 49–60.

Bey, Marquis. "How Ya Mama'n'em? Blackness, Nonbinariness, and Radical Subjectivity." *Peitho: Journal of the Coalition of Feminist Scholars in the History of Rhetoric and Composition* 22, no. 4 (Summer 2020): n.p. https://cfshrc.org/article/how-ya-mamanem-blackness-nonbinariness-and-radical-subjectivity/.

Bey, Marquis. "RE: [No Subject]—On Nonbinary Gender." *Qui Parle: Critical Humanities and Social Sciences* 30, no. 2 (2021): 229–47.

Bjorkman, Bronwyn M. "Singular *They* and the Syntactic Representation of Gender in English." *Glossa: A Journal of General Linguistics* 2, no. 1 (2017): 80.

Blanchard, Sessi Kuwabara. "In Defense of the Trans Villainess." Them, September 2, 2018. https://www.them.us/story/in-defense-of-the-trans-villainess.

Brand, Dionne. *The Blue Clerk: Ars Poetica in 59 Versos*. Durham, NC: Duke University Press, 2018.

Briggs, Laura. "These Are Not My People." *Ms*. Magazine, January 7, 2019. https://msmagazine.com/2019/01/07/these-are-not-my-people/.

Butler, Judith. *Bodies That Matter: On the Discursive Limits of "Sex."* New York: Routledge, 1993.

Butler, Judith. "Conscience Doth Make Subjects of Us All." *Yale French Studies*, no. 88 (1995): 6–26.

Carter, J. Kameron. "Black Malpractice (A Poetics of the Sacred)." *Social Text* 37, no. 2 (2019): 67–107.

Carter, J. Kameron. *Race: A Theological Account*. Oxford: Oxford University Press, 2008.

Chambers-Letson, Joshua. *After the Party: A Manifesto for Queer of Color Life*. New York: NYU Press, 2018.

Chaudhry, V. Varun. "Trans/Coalitional Love-Politics: Black Feminisms and the Radical Possibilities of Transgender Studies." *TSQ: Transgender Studies Quarterly* 6, no. 4 (2019): 521–38.

Chen, Jian Neo. *Trans Exploits: Trans of Color Cultures and Technologies in Movement*. Durham, NC: Duke University Press, 2018.

Collins, Patricia Hill. *Black Feminist Thought: Knowledge, Consciousness, and the Politics of Empowerment*. London: Routledge, 2000.

Conrad, Joseph. *Heart of Darkness*. New York: W. W. Norton, 2016.

Crawley, Ashon. "Stayed | Freedom | Hallelujah." In *Otherwise Worlds: Against Settler Colonialism and Anti-Blackness*, edited by Tiffany Lethabo King, Jenell Navarro, and Andrea Smith, 27–37. Durham, NC: Duke University Press, 2020.

Critchley, Simon. "Being and Time, Part 4: Thrown into This World." *Guardian*, June 29, 2009. https://www.theguardian.com/commentisfree/belief/2009/jun/29/religion-philosophy.

Detournay, Diane. "The Racial Life of 'Cisgender': Reflections on Sex, Gender and the Body." *Parallax* 25, no. 1 (2019): 58–74.

Devereaux, Shaadi. "Rollersets and Realness: Black Womanhood Defined as Drag Performance." *Black Girl Dangerous* (blog), July 24, 2014. https://www.bgdblog.org/2014/07/rollersets-realness-black-womanhood-defined-drag-performance/.

Enke, Anne, ed. *Transfeminist Perspectives in and Beyond Transgender and Gender Studies*. Philadelphia: Temple University Press, 2012.

Ferber, Alona. "Judith Butler on the Culture Wars, JK Rowling, and Living in 'Anti-Intellectual Times.'" *New Statesman*, September 22, 2020. https://www

.newstatesman.com/international/2020/09/judith-butler-culture-wars-jk-rowling-and-living-anti-intellectual-times.

Gibson, Andrea. *Lord of the Butterflies*. Minneapolis, MN: button poetry, 2018.

Gill-Peterson, Jules. "Communist Christine Jorgensen and the MILFs." Sad Brown Girl, February 12, 2021. https://sadbrowngirl.substack.com/p/communist-christine-jorgensen-and?s=r.

Giovannitti, Sophia. "In Defense of Men: On the Failures of Political Heterosexuality and No Cis Men." Majuscule. Accessed February 2, 2022. https://majusculelit.com/in-defense-of-men/.

Gossett, Reina, Eric A. Stanley, and Johanna Burton, eds. *Trap Door: Trans Cultural Production and the Politics of Visibility*. Cambridge, MA: MIT Press, 2017.

Gray, Rae. "Pistols or Pearls: Gender Reveal Parties Are a Sham." Bitch Media, November 6, 2017. https://www.bitchmedia.org/article/gender-reveal-parties-phenomenon.

Green, Kai M. "The Essential I/Eye in We: A Black TransFeminist Approach to Ethnographic Film." *Black Camera* 6, no. 2 (2015): 187–200.

Green, Kai M. "'Race and Gender Are Not the Same!' Is Not a Good Response to the 'Transracial'/Transgender Question OR We Can and Must Do Better." The Feminist Wire, June 14, 2015. http://www.thefeministwire.com/2015/06/race-and-gender-are-not-the-same-is-not-a-good-response-to-the-transracial-transgender-question-or-we-can-and-must-do-better/.

Gutting, Gary. *French Philosophy in the Twentieth Century*. New York: Cambridge University Press, 2001.

Halberstam, Jack. *The Queer Art of Failure*. Durham, NC: Duke University Press, 2011.

Halberstam, Jack. *Trans*: A Quick and Quirky Account of Gender Variability*. Oakland: University of California Press, 2018.

Halberstam, Jack. "Unbuilding Gender." *Places Journal*, October 2018. https://doi.org/10.22269/181003.

Hardt, Michael, and Antonio Negri. *Assembly*. Oxford: Oxford University Press, 2017.

Hayward, Eva. "More Lessons from a Starfish: Prefixial Flesh and Transspeciated Selves." *Women's Studies Quarterly* 36, nos. 3–4 (2008): 64–85.

Hayward, Eva, and Che Gossett. "Impossibility of That." *Angelaki* 22, no. 2 (2017): 15–24.

Henderson, Kevin. "Becoming Lesbian: Monique Wittig's Queer-Trans-Feminism." *Journal of Lesbian Studies* 22, no. 2 (2018): 185–203.

Hess, Amanda. "Who's 'They'?" *New York Times*, March 29, 2016. https://www.nytimes.com/2016/04/03/magazine/whos-they.html.

Horton-Stallings, LaMonda. *Funk the Erotic: Transaesthetics and Black Sexual Cultures*. Urbana: University of Illinois Press, 2015.

Huxtable, Juliana. *Mucous in My Pineal Gland*. New York: Capricious, 2017.

Kaba, Mariame. "A Jailbreak of the Imagination: Seeing Prisons for What They Are and Demanding Transformation." Truthout, May 3, 2018. https://truthout.org/articles/a-jailbreak-of-the-imagination-seeing-prisons-for-what-they-are-and-demanding-transformation/.

Keegan, Cáel M. *Lana and Lilly Wachowski*. Urbana: University of Illinois Press, 2018.

Kelley, Robin, and Fred Moten. "Do Black Lives Matter? A Conversation between Robin Kelley and Fred Moten." Dr. Lester K. Spence, 2014. Accessed January 22, 2015. https://www.lesterspence.com/do-black-lives-matter-a-conversation-between-robin-kelley-and-fred-moten/.

King, Tiffany Lethabo. *The Black Shoals: Offshore Formations of Black and Native Studies*. Durham, NC: Duke University Press, 2019.

Krell, Elías Cosenza. "Is Transmisogyny Killing Trans Women of Color?: Black Trans Feminisms and the Exigencies of White Femininity." *TSQ: Transgender Studies Quarterly* 4, no. 2 (2017): 226–42.

Leo, Brooklyn. "The Colonial/Modern [Cis]Gender System and Trans World Traveling." *Hypatia: A Journal of Feminist Philosophy* 35, no. 3 (Summer 2020): 454–74.

Lugones, María. "The Coloniality of Gender." In *The Palgrave Handbook of Gender and Development*, edited by Wendy Harcourt, 13–33. London: Palgrave Macmillan, 2016.

Malatino, Hil. *Trans Care*. Minneapolis: University of Minnesota Press, 2020.

Manic Focus. "Joy in the Noise." Track 3 from *Minds Rising*. Label Engine, 2017. MP3.

Marcuse, Herbert. *Negations: Essays in Critical Theory*. Translated by Jeremy J. Shapiro. London: MayFly, 2017.

Martel, James R. *The Misinterpellated Subject*. Durham, NC: Duke University Press, 2017.

Mock, Janet. *Redefining Realness: My Path to Womanhood, Identity, Love and So Much More*. New York: Atria Books, 2014.

Moten, Fred. "Blackness and Nothingness (Mysticism in the Flesh)." *SAQ: South Atlantic Quarterly* 112, no. 4 (2013): 737–80.

Moten, Fred. "Black Op." *PMLA* 123, no. 5 (2008): 1743–47.

Moten, Fred. "Come On, Get It!" *The New Inquiry*, February 19, 2018. https://thenewinquiry.com/come_on_get_it/.

Moten, Fred. "Ensemble: An Interview with Dr. Fred Moten." Interview by Nehal El-Hadi. MICE Magazine, June 6, 2018. http://micemagazine.ca/issue-four/ensemble-interview-dr-fred-moten.

Moten, Fred. *Stolen Life*. Durham, NC: Duke University Press, 2018.

Nash, Jennifer. *Black Feminism Reimagined*. Durham, NC: Duke University Press, 2018.

Nelson, Maggie. *The Argonauts*. Minneapolis: Graywolf, 2015.

Offman, Hilary. "Queering of a Cisgender Psychoanalyst." *TSQ: Transgender Studies Quarterly* 4, nos. 3–4 (2017): 405–20.

Phoenix, Lola. "Gender Abolition as Colonisation." Medium, December 26, 2015. https://medium.com/gender-2-0/gender-abolition-as-colonisation-f32b55505e38.

Rajunov, Micah, and A. Scott Duane, eds. *Nonbinary: Memoirs of Gender and Identity*. New York: Columbia University Press, 2019.

Richardson, Matt. *The Queer Limit of Black Memory: Black Lesbian Literature and Irresolution*. Columbus: Ohio State University Press, 2016.

Riley, Denise. *Am I That Name? Feminism and the Category of "Women" in History*. Minneapolis: University of Minnesota Press, 1988.

Roche, Juno. *Trans Power: Own Your Gender*. Philadelphia: Jessica Kingsley, 2019.

Rosenberg, Jordy. *Confessions of the Fox*. New York: One World, 2019.

ross, kihana miraya. "Call It What It Is: Anti-Blackness." *New York Times*, June 4, 2020. https://www.nytimes.com/2020/06/04/opinion/george-floyd-anti-blackness.html.

Salamon, Gayle. *Assuming a Body: Transgender and Rhetorics of Materiality*. New York: Columbia University Press, 2010.

Salamon, Gayle. "'The Place Where Life Hides Away': Merleau-Ponty, Fanon, and the Location of Bodily Being." *Differences* 17, no. 2 (2006): 96–112.

Santana, Dora Silva. "Transitionings and Returnings: Experiments with the Poetics of Transatlantic Water." *TSQ: Transgender Studies Quarterly* 4, no. 2 (2017): 181–90.

Scheman, Naomi. *Shifting Ground: Knowledge and Reality, Transgression and Trustworthiness*. Oxford: Oxford University Press, 2011.

Sexton, Jared. *Black Men, Black Feminism: Lucifer's Nocturne*. New York: Springer Berlin Heidelberg, 2018.

Seymour, Richard. "None Shall Pass: Trans and the Rewriting of the Body." Salvage. March 14, 2017. http://salvage.zone/in-print/none-shall-pass-trans-and-the-rewriting-of-the-body/.

Sigel, Beanie. *Remember Them Days*. Roc-A-Fella Records, 2000.

Silva, Denise Ferreira da. *Toward a Global Idea of Race*. Minneapolis: University of Minnesota Press, 2007.

Silva Santana, Dora. "Transitionings and Returnings: Experiments with the Poetics of Transatlantic Water." *TSQ: Transgender Studies Quarterly* 4, no. 2 (2017): 181–90.

Snorton, C. Riley. *Black on Both Sides: A Racial History of Trans Identity*. Minneapolis: University of Minnesota Press, 2017.

Solanas, Valerie. *SCUM Manifesto*. Oakland: AK, 2013.

Soldier Phoenix. "So Is Frieza Gay." IGN Boards, May 19, 2014. https://www.ignboards.com/threads/so-is-frieza-gay.453993169/.

Spillers, Hortense. "Mama's Baby, Papa's Maybe: An American Grammar Book." *Diacritics* 17, no. 2 (1987): 65–81.

Stanley, Eric A., and Nat Smith, eds. *Captive Genders: Trans Embodiment and the Prison Industrial Complex*. Oakland, CA: AK, 2011.

Stein, Jordan Alexander. *Avidly Reads Theory*. New York: NYU Press, 2019.

Steinbock, Eliza. *Shimmering Images: Trans Cinema, Embodiment, and the Aesthetics of Change*. Durham, NC: Duke University Press, 2019.

Stryker, Susan. "The Transgender Issue: An Introduction." *GLQ: A Journal of Lesbian and Gay Studies* 4, no. 2 (1998): 145–58.

Stryker, Susan. "Transgender Studies: Queer Theory's Evil Twin." *GLQ: A Journal of Lesbian and Gay Studies* 10, no. 2 (2004): 212–15.

Stryker, Susan, Paisley Currah, and Lisa Jean Moore. "Introduction: Trans-, Trans, or Transgender?" *WSQ: Women's Studies Quarterly* 36, no. 3 (2008): 11–22. https://doi.org/10.1353/wsq.0.0112.

Stryker, Susan, and Stephen Whittle. *The Transgender Studies Reader*. New York: Routledge, 2013.

Thom, Kai Cheng. *Fierce Femmes and Notorious Liars: A Dangerous Trans Girl's Confabulous Memoir*. Montreal: Metonymy, 2016.

Thom, Kai Cheng. *I Hope We Choose Love: A Trans Girl's Notes from the End of the World*. Vancouver: Arsenal Pulp, 2019.

Tinsley, Omise'eke Natasha. "Black Atlantic, Queer Atlantic: Queer Imaginings of the Middle Passage." *GLQ: A Journal of Lesbian and Gay Studies* 14, nos. 2–3 (2008): 191–215.

Tourmaline, Eric, A. Stanley, and Johanna Burton, eds. *Trap Door: Trans Cultural Production and the Politics of Visibility*. Cambridge, MA: MIT Press, 2017.

Wark, McKenzie. "The Many-Handed Hunger of Transsexuality: On T. Fleischmann." Public Seminar, October 21, 2019. http://publicseminar.org/essays/the-many-handed-hunger-of-transsexuality/.

Wark, McKenzie. *Reverse Cowgirl*. South Pasadena, CA: Semiotext(e), 2020.
Warren, Calvin. "Calling into Being: Tranifestation, Black Trans, and the Problem of Ontology." *TSQ: Transgender Studies Quarterly* 4, no. 2 (2017): 266–74.
Weber, Bruce. "Leslie Feinberg, Writer and Transgender Activist, Dies at 65." *New York Times*, November 24, 2014. https://www.nytimes.com/2014/11/25/nyregion/leslie-feinberg-writer-and-transgender-activist-dies-at-65.html.
Wilchins, Riki. *TRANS/Gressive: How Transgender Activists Took on Gay Rights, Feminism, the Media and Congress . . . and Won!* Riverdale, NY: Riverdale Avenue, 2017.
Wilchins, Riki Anne. *Read My Lips: Sexual Subversion and the End of Gender*. Ithaca, NY: Firebrand, 1997.
Woolf, Virginia. *The Waves*. New York: Harvest Books, 1978.
Zadjermann, Paule, dir. *Judith Butler: Philosophical Encounters of the Third Kind*. Brooklyn, NY: First Run/Icarus Films, 2006.
Ziyad, Hari. "My Gender Is Black." Afropunk, July 12, 2017. https://afropunk.com/2017/07/my-gender-is-black/.
Zurn, Perry. "The Politics of Anonymity: Foucault, Feminism, and Gender Non-Conforming Prisoners." *PhiloSOPHIA* 6, no. 1 (2016): 27–48.

# INDEX